Birds

Divine Messengers

Birds

Divine Messengers

Transform your Life with
their Guidance and Wisdom

Andrea Wansbury

FINDHORN
Press

© Andrea Wansbury 2006

First published by Findhorn Press in 2006

ISBN 1-84409-074-4

British Library Cataloguing-in-Publication Data.
A catalogue record for this book is available
from the British Library.

Edited by Jean Semrau

Cover design by Damian Keenan

Interior design by Pam Bochel

Printed by WS Bookwell, Finland

Published by
Findhorn Press
305a The Park, Findhorn
Forres IV36 3TE
Scotland, UK

tel 01309 690582/fax 690036
info@findhornpress.com
www.findhornpress.com

In loving memory of Gypsy
(2000–2005)

Table of Contents

The eagle loves to soar high above the world,
not to look down on people,
but in order to encourage them to look up.

Elizabeth Kübler-Ross,
The Wheel of Life

Prologue

"Even the merest gesture is holy if it is filled with faith."

Franz Kafka (1883–1924), Czech writer

Many years ago, I went to the local veterinary clinic to collect a prescription for a friend's cat, and as I walked in through the door I found a heated discussion going on at the desk. A farmer had brought in a week-old duckling for the vet to put down because it had been born deformed, but the vet was hesitant to comply with the farmer's wishes because the baby duck was in no pain and seemed to have a lot of spunk. They continued to argue until, to everyone's amazement including my own, I said I would take the duckling home and look after him. It was obvious from the relief shown on their faces that I had saved the day, but the vet did say that the duck, with his spastic legs, two stumps for wings and a genetically weak heart, would never be able to walk or fly, and would probably not live longer than two or three weeks.

Still wondering what had possessed me to make such an impulsive offer, I took my new acquisition home and decided I would make the last couple of weeks of this baby duck's life his best. I gave him the name of Orville and spent the next few days digging a pond and building a comfortable shelter at the bottom of my garden, using an old, large tin bath as a temporary pond until the permanent one was in place. It was the start of many a loving hour with my duck. Every morning and evening, before and after work, I would sit with Orville in my lap, and as I stroked his feathers and chatted to him, I enjoyed watching his little eyes close, as if in seventh heaven, as I showered him with the love and adoration I genuinely felt. I hadn't bothered to enclose his pen because his disabilities didn't allow him to move far and, strangely, I wasn't worried about neighbours' cats getting to him. He never seemed lonely, because there were always garden birds sitting with him, or helping themselves to his food.

Six months passed, and Orville grew into a beautiful white bird, outliving the vet's prediction of a two-week life expectancy. But his deformities remained and he still couldn't walk or fly, and could only manage an awkward rolling shuffle between his shelter and the pond close by. But I didn't regret my decision about taking on this disabled duck: I knew he wasn't in any pain, he had become a much-loved pet, and, I reasoned, if he was not happy he wouldn't have lived as long as he had. Then one day Orville accomplished a feat beyond anybody's wildest expectations.

Early one summer's evening I heard loud quacking noises coming from outside the back door, and when I opened it, there was Orville sitting at the back door step trying to get my attention. Astonished, I looked at him, then to his open pen down at the other end of the garden, and I was momentarily lost for words while I tried to take in what had happened. I didn't know how he managed it, or how long it took, but he had somehow walked all the way from his pen to the back door, a distance of about fifteen yards. I swooped him up in my arms and, with tears in my eyes, cuddled him for a long time before carrying him back to his pen.

It didn't stop there. From that day onwards, Orville forgot all about his disabilities and made it his mission to take a walk everyday to visit some part of the big garden, regardless of his buckled spastic legs and no wings to help with balance. The vet said he would never walk, and here was my duck marching all over the garden! I felt so proud of him, even when he discovered my vegetable patch and regularly helped himself to my spinach and carrot tops. The vet didn't believe me when I told him, and many of my friends came round to see for themselves in case I was exaggerating. Orville was the epitome of a happy ending to a classic fairytale.

In this book, I will explain how every bird is a divine messenger, each one carrying a specific message of wisdom, guidance or encouragement, to help us on our spiritual paths. The message a duck brings is FAITH.

Orville didn't just bring the message of faith – he demonstrated it too. He proved that, with faith, one can achieve anything in life, despite the odds, and that if we believe in ourselves enough, no matter what outside opinions are thrown at us or what obstacles are put in our way, we can achieve the seemingly impossible.

When I first brought Orville home, I must admit that for a few days I wondered if I had done the right thing and whether it would have been kinder to have had him put down. But now, I thank God for bringing Orville into my life and teaching me the valuable lesson of faith. His message has had a long-lasting effect on me because, whenever any fear or doubt has crept into my mind that has threatened to hold me back on my spiritual journey, I think of Orville and what can be achieved when we empower ourselves with faith; as a result, my belief in myself and in my abilities is steadily growing.

Orville lived a happy and fulfilled life for over two years before finally succumbing to his weak heart. I buried him, with much ceremony and tears, under the loquat tree in the back garden. For over two months afterwards, I noticed that no wild bird came near the loquat tree. It was as if the other birds were respecting and honoring the passing of a loved and cherished colleague.

An Ostrich Eye and a Cuban Bee Humming Bird drawn to scale

(*The former is the largest living bird in the world, the latter is the smallest*)

Introduction

"...through every star, through every blade of grass, is not God made visible if we will open our minds and eyes?"

Thomas Carlyle (1795–1881), Scottish essayist
and historian

Have you ever felt how still, calm and peaceful it is between the hours of midnight and about four in the morning? This is the time when Mother Earth is healing, the time when she is absorbing all the negativity generated during the day and transforming it into the positive energies that are conducive to all life. Then, as the first rays of sunlight appear over the horizon, the birds begin their dawn chorus, signalling that the night's healing is complete and a new day has begun.

I don't think we appreciate how powerful Mother Earth is, and how much we rely on her for our well-being. We take it for granted that the sun will rise in the morning, the air will be filled with oxygen, the rain will fall, and everything we plant will grow. Our blasé attitude causes us to chop down trees, dig huge mines deep into the bowels of the earth, pollute the air with emissions from industrial factories and cars, and destroy the ecology by constructing roads and building complexes, all without a moment's thought of the subsequent implications on our lives. Upsetting the balance of the natural world has been due not only to human avarice, but also to human ignorance. We have forgotten that we are part of, and connected to, Nature in every conceivable way, which means that whatever goes on in the natural world will automatically have a ripple effect on us humans, and vice versa.

There is a vast sea of energy that unites all of creation, an eternally-flowing matrix that never depletes. It is called *prana* in Indian Sanskrit, *chi* in China, *ki* in Japan, and *life force* in the Western world. By whatever name this energy goes, it emanates from one source – the Divine. This life force surrounds and permeates all living matter; it keeps us alive and bonds all of life together. Scientists describe life on earth as a universal hologram, where the whole is made up of individual parts, with each individual part containing the whole. In other words, we are individuals, but we are not separate. By becoming aware of this "no separation", as the Zen masters call it, we realize that the life force that sustains a tree, for example, is no different from our own.

The idea that we are somehow connected to every living thing by a common energy seems strange to many people. Yet we have all experienced the sense of upliftment when we stand next to a cascading waterfall or the crashing waves of the sea, and we know we feel more happy and energetic when the sun is shining, and more miserable when it is overcast. We choose to go to the mountains, to the woods or to the coast for our annual vacations in order to unwind, and come away feeling rejuvenated. We might not understand that the higher vibrating energies of the unadulterated natural world infuse with our own energies, enhancing them and pulling them up, to leave us feeling restored and happy, but we are certainly aware that being in the company of Nature makes us feel more alive.

Ancient cultures understood this connection with Nature, and they knew how to live in harmony with the natural cycles. They saw the Divine in everything, from the tiniest pebble to the largest mountain; they listened and took note of what Nature had to say, because they knew that Nature's wisdom is divine wisdom. As time went on, however, we began to see ourselves as isolated from everything around us, and as a result we lost touch, and became out of sync, with the natural world. We did not realise that by setting ourselves apart from Nature we were also separating ourselves from God. Nature is a timeless support system, not only for our physical life, but for our mental, emotional and spiritual well-being, as well. Divine wisdom and spiritual values are reflected in all aspects of the natural world, reinforcing the principle, "As above, so below", or, "Thy will be done on earth as it is in heaven".

Nature reminds us of the physical, emotional, mental and spiritual aspects of ourselves. For example, trees are supported and sustained by the roots they send deep into the earth, reminding us that we too have an energetic root system that anchors us to the earth, through which we are supported and sustained by the energies of Mother Earth. Seeds that are planted in the ground germinate and give rise to new plants, reflecting the seeds of thought that we sow in our minds that germinate and produce our physical reality, the harvest of which can be weeds or beautiful flowers, depending on the quality of the seeds planted. The oceans reflect the high water constituent of our bodies that keeps us functioning healthily. The rivers represent the blood and lymphatic systems in our bodies that carry nutrients and unwanted products to and from our cells, and just as it is important to keep our rivers flowing and free from pollution, so it is important for us to keep these bodily systems free from chemical and negative emotional debris. The changing seasons reflect back to us the continuation of life through birth, death and rebirth, and are indicative not only of the continual dying and renewal of all the cells in our bodies but also of the understanding that when physical death comes, it isn't final but is immediately followed by rebirth in another realm. The rain cleanses the earth just as crying cleanses our bodies; a rainbow reflects back to us the same seven colors as the spinning vortices (chakras) in the energy fields that surround our physical bodies; and a morning dewdrop is in essence the same as a baby's tear. The list is endless.

Because we have forgotten that we are connected to Nature, we have forgotten that the Divine often speaks to us and guides us through this medium. There are messages in the stars and planets, from crystals and the mineral world, from the animal, bird and plant kingdoms, from dreams, from angels and spirit guides, and from other humans.

Many books have been written about crystals, astrology, dreams, flower remedies and so on, but as far as I know, none exclusively on the spiritual role birds play – yet birds are very much a part of the intricate network of spiritual teachers found in the natural world. Throughout history, birds have been a source of inspiration in helping humans to understand the physical and spiritual implications of living life on earth. Birds symbolise the spiritual nature of man by reflecting, among other things, our spiritual aspirations, our intuitive abilities, and our ability to rise above our fears and limitations; in the process, they teach us Divine principles.

In addition, birds have the unique role of being personal Divine messengers.

When I began to study birds from an esoteric point of view, I soon realized that there is a specific message, or keyword, attached to every species of bird. Each bird acts as a messenger for God by bringing to us its own individual message at a time when we most need to hear guidance. These messages are words of wisdom and advice, and they can help us to identify talents we are not using, or the negative beliefs and thought patterns that are holding us back. Once these messages are understood and applied to our lives, they can be a valuable source of direction as we progress on our spiritual journeys.

I have written this book to take you into the magical world of birds, because it is time for us to understand, once more, this wonderful aspect of nature. I want to share with you their spiritual teachings and the spiritual wisdom they bring, but I also want to reawaken the knowledge that birds are Divine messengers. The individual messages of each species of bird written in this book are derived from spiritual guidance through my own intuition, although a few of the messages are already more universally known, such as the dove bringing its message of peace, the eagle bringing its message of power, and the swan with its message of transformation. At the end of the book I have given a list of the messages or keywords of nearly one hundred different birds found worldwide.

Let us now enter into the intriguing world of birds because, the more we come to understand the messages of birds, the more intimately we'll come to know ourselves.

Chapter One
Feathered Friends

"I would rather live in a world where my life is surrounded by mystery than live in a world so small that my mind could comprehend it."

Harry Emerson Fosdick (1878–1969),
American clergyman and professor

Ever since I was a little girl I have been sensitive to the energies around me. I usually kept any psychic impressions to myself, though, because I didn't know how to explain what I was feeling in satisfactory words, and when I did try it was usually met with looks that ranged from wide-eyed fear and narrow-eyed suspicion, to eyes raised upwards in utter disbelief. I had plenty of friends, a happy home and wonderful times, but I secretly wished I had someone with whom to share my inner world of unusual phenomena. I didn't understand why people referred to these things as abnormal when it was to me the most natural thing in the world. I certainly wasn't unique, even though it felt like it at times, but in those days esoteric matters tended to be an enigma and were not understood in the ways they are today, so it was better to keep quiet. From the nuns at the convent school I attended, I knew about the guardian angels that were watching over us, but that wasn't quite the same as having somebody in solid human form in which to confide.

When I was three years old my parents took me to the London Zoo for the first time. They had planned to make it a whole day's outing with lunch and tea, but I marched round the zoo as fast as I could before firmly declaring I'd had enough and wanted to go home. My parents were surprised by my lack of enthusiasm, but what I couldn't explain to them was that I hated being in the confines of the zoo because I was beginning to feel overwhelmed by the sense of unhappiness and despair of the animals, especially the mammals, from being in surroundings far removed from their natural habitat. Their combined sadness nearly became too much for me.

A few years later an aunt and uncle took my sister, our cousins and me to see the circus when it came to a nearby town. I can't say I enjoyed it much, and when the performing elephants came into the ring, I excused myself and went outside. There, I came across a huge brown bear lying in a cage, and when I looked into its eyes, I was shocked to see how lifeless they were – it was if the very light of its soul had been extinguished. Those two seemingly dead eyes haunted my dreams for many nights afterwards, and I used to lie awake for hours devising ways to sneak back to the circus after dark to let all the caged animals free. Thankfully, for the town's safety, these plans were never put into action.

Being in tune with the energies around me didn't always tug at my heartstrings. I saw magic in rainbows, in sunsets and in the misty early mornings of autumn, and the sounds of a babbling brook or a crackling log fire, or the smell of newly mown hay, never failed to lift my spirits. But this was not the sort of thing to let on to your fellow schoolmates if you wanted to keep your credibility. So I played it safe and didn't mention my feelings for the natural world, instead joining them in their less than riveting discussions on the merits of the latest pop idol, and why mascara always left your eyelashes clumped together.

I have always had a particular love for pine trees. As a child I enjoyed the walks my family took through a nearby dense pine forest. I remember running ahead as fast as I could, to put enough distance between my family and me so I could be by myself for a while. I wanted to savor the forest on my own, and as I leant against the huge trees with my eyes closed, breathing in the wonderful smell of pine resin, I would literally begin to feel myself floating away to another realm where everything was serene and nothing else mattered. The energy of the pine trees made me feel alive and, more importantly, made me feel I belonged. Years later I read that the energies of a pine tree pulsate at a very similar rate to that of the human energy field, and being in close proximity to these trees recharges your energies, which only confirmed what I already knew.

In my formative years, I was surrounded by countryside, so it was no wonder I developed a love for Nature. I grew up in a little village in England, on the outskirts of London, that dates back to Saxon times; not only did the family home back on to fields and woods, but the village is surrounded on one side by a vast meadow that stretches all the way to neighbouring villages. Every year our summer vacations were spent at a remote cottage on the Isle of Wight where every day we would take long walks through the countryside or along deserted shores. The cottage itself was set in acres of ground, with old fir trees standing like sentinels in the front, and an apple orchard and woods behind; in the distance were rolling hills or the sea, depending on which way you faced. Every morning I would get up very early so I could stand on the verandah and take in the sights and sounds around me. To this day, the aroma of sweet peas permeating the air, the rustling sound of the gentle wind blowing through the needles of the old firs, and the call of the wood pigeon, will always transport me back to those carefree times.

My father inspired my enthusiasm for birds, and he taught me from a young age how to recognize each garden bird by its call, as well as the ecological importance of birds. For as long as I can remember, he has had numerous bird-feeders in his garden, all strategically placed out of reach of foxes, squirrels, and neighbour's cats, and each containing different seeds or nuts to attract a variety of birds. My parents are also very keen and skilful gardeners, so their garden deliberately contains all sorts of berried shrubs that are known to attract birds. It is sad to think that certain garden birds are declining in numbers due to the modern use of pesticides and increasing land development. As a small child, I loved looking out of the kitchen window first thing in the morning to see the seemingly endless line of house sparrows sitting on the washing line and along the garden fences, all waiting for the seed that was about to be hand-strewn around the lawn for their benefit. Unfortunately, this once prolific little garden bird is rare to see in London nowadays.

One of my favorite movies when I was growing up was "Mary Poppins", not only because the late Victorian and early Edwardian era in London has always fascinated me, but also because I would have given anything to have had a Nanny who could perform magic. I also loved the fictional old lady who sat on the steps of St. Paul's cathedral in London, feeding the birds and encouraging the public to do the same by selling seed at "tuppence a bag". I sat on the steps of St. Paul's once and no bird ever came near me, much to my chagrin, but it was a different story standing in Trafalgar Square. In the shadow of Nelson's column, we children would stand with outstretched hands holding seed bought from the vendors, waiting with a mixture of exhilaration and trepidation for the onslaught of pigeons to land on our arms and heads.

On trips to our local park my mother would always take my sister and me to see the bird aviary that bordered a little tea garden. The birds included parakeets, budgerigars, finches and canaries, with the ultimate attraction of a cockatoo from Australia with the original name of Cocky.

House Sparrow

I dutifully walked from cage to cage, but I could never muster up much enthusiasm because I didn't like the artificiality of it all. The cages had plenty of fresh air, water and seed, but dead branches rising up from the concrete floors, along with a few wooden rods protruding from the walls for perches, demonstrated to me an unnatural habitat for birds. My father, however, explained that these birds had been bred in captivity and, if they were released back into the wild, they wouldn't last long, as their natural instincts for survival were long forgotten. As if to prove a point, Cocky lived to be well over forty years of age in captivity.

I have always disliked caged birds and animals, but it was only recently that I realized the reason went much deeper than just empathizing with the bird or animal. One of my biggest fears in this life is losing my own freedom, feeling trapped and confined, and when I see a caged animal or bird, it is reflecting back to me this fear.

When I emigrated to South Africa I took the familial love of birds with me. It was fun learning the names of the new garden birds around me in Johannesburg, and trying to remember which call went with which bird. Gone were the blackbirds, wrens and magpies of England, replaced by bokmakeries, bulbuls, and paradise flycatchers. The African birds seemed almost exotic to me compared with the English birds, but

I soon learned that decorative plumage was not necessarily an indication of a colorful song. The essentially plain English blackbird has the most beautiful song, whereas the decorative crested barbet of Africa, scruffily clad in feathers of yellow, black, red and white, is certainly not a chorister, uttering a monotonous sound like an alarm clock ringing from beneath a pillow. Another case in point is the lilac-breasted roller found mainly in the northern parts of South Africa. Its colorful splendor is marked by the white, green and rust on its head and back, its lilac throat and breast, and the turquoise and electric blue underparts, but its call is a rather unattractive series of harsh squawks. A beautiful bird until it opens its beak!

During the first few years in Johannesburg, I used to watch the European swallows gather on the telephone lines in March, ready for their mass migration to summer climes in the Northern Hemisphere. It seemed to take days for them to assemble, but as soon as they left I would write to my father in England giving him their "date of departure", and within a couple of weeks Dad would write back to say they had arrived. Obviously this isn't to say they were the same birds, because we didn't officially tag them or used any other form of identification; we just had fun monitoring, in a layperson's way, the fascinating migratory movement of the swallows.

One thing I have really enjoyed in South Africa is visiting the game reserves, where wild animals roam freely in their natural habitat within the perimeters of the reserves. I don't think I have a particular favorite reserve because each one has its own topographical beauty. The game reserve I have frequented the most is the Kruger National Park, the first big wildlife reserve in Africa, covering nearly 1,950,000 hectares.[1] Many tourists visit the park with the sole purpose of wanting to see the wild animals, particularly the "Big Five" – elephant, rhinoceros, lion, leopard and buffalo – and sometimes they come away disappointed because they haven't spotted much animal wildlife at all. But with over 450 different species, the bird life is always abundant.[2] Whenever I have visited any of the national game reserves, my friends and I make it our priority to see how many different birds we can spot in any one day; it makes each trip much more enjoyable, for any viewing of game is an added bonus, and we never come away feeling as if a whole day were wasted.

There are some people who take bird-watching very seriously and are nicknamed "twitchers". A couple of years ago when my mother was visiting me, we spent the day at the Witwatersrand National Botanical Gardens (now called the Walter Sisulu Botanical Gardens) in

Johannesburg, well-known for its magnificent gardens, huge waterfall, and a resident family of wild black eagles. After lunch, we decided to go to the bird hide, a small hut concealed among the trees and overlooking a large lake, that is purposely built for bird-spotting while being hidden from view. As we stepped inside, surrounded by notices to "Keep Quiet", we came across a couple of twitchers who were already ensconced in the hide, notebooks open and binoculars trained on the outside vista for the slightest ruffle of wings. My mom, trying to look the part, sat down with the binoculars and began studiously to scan the lake, then whispered to me that the mountain in the background seemed strangely small and far away. I whispered back that she was looking through the wrong end of the binoculars. With that, the two of us began to giggle, and the more we tried to be quiet, the more hysterical we became. Eventually, it became too much for the twitchers, and mumbling something under their breath about how some people just didn't know when to be serious, they snatched up their twitchers' paraphernalia and strutted out of the hide in a huff. When they had left, my mother and I collapsed into loud fits of laughter that would have frightened off even the tamest bird.

Up until that point, birds had been an enjoyable adjunct in my life. I enjoyed bird spotting in the national parks, and I loved watching and feeding the garden birds and listening to their familiar calls and songs. But one day, something extraordinary happened that made me realize that birds were a lot more than just a pleasant pastime. I began to discover that birds were divine spiritual messengers and, by the very nature of their symbolic meanings, were there to help us understand the nuances of life in our quest for spiritual growth.

Suddenly, my study of birds became serious.

Chapter Two
Spiritual Communicators

"God has delegated himself to a million deputies."

Ralph Waldo Emerson (1803–1882),
American essayist and poet

Susan came to see me in my capacity as an allied medical professional, for help with a painful lower back. Conventional treatment wasn't proving very successful so, with her permission, we decided to switch gears and turn our attention to energy medicine. As our healing sessions progressed, we began to discuss the energy blockages I had picked up and how they related to her physical symptoms. I also asked her to keep a daily journal in which to document her feelings, any changes in her condition, and other details that might be pertinent to her healing. I insisted she kept the journal because I knew Susan was a person who loathed to focus any attention on herself and this was a good way of making her the center of attraction in her own life. Every session started with a report back, which enabled us to discuss what came up and how it related to her path of healing. For example, past memories were suddenly remembered at odd times, provoking emotive responses; she started having nosebleeds (her way of unconsciously releasing pent-up emotions) and she developed a feeling of a "hole" in the sole of one foot from which she felt the pain swirling out of her body when she was in bed at night.

It was one Monday morning, two weeks into her healing sessions, that Susan reported some curious events that had happened to her over the weekend, all involving birds. It began on the Friday night with a vivid dream in which she dreamed of hundreds of very brightly colored sunbirds flying around her head while three owls sat on a branch next to her. Susan said she didn't feel frightened or overwhelmed in the dream, as the sunbirds seemed almost gentle and tranquil in the way they fluttered around her, and their bright shimmering colors reminded her of a kaleidoscope. She did find strange, though, the presence of the three owls sedately sitting beside her.

The next day Susan attended a function out of town, and as she was driving back home that night she noticed a crowned plover flying next to her car in line with her passenger window. It flew with her for some way, and when she reached her home, the plover landed nearby and seemed to wait until she was safely in the driveway and the gates shut behind her, before flying off. It was if the plover were escorting her home, keeping a watch to make sure no harm came to her. As soon as she was in the house, Susan duly wrote about the incident in her journal.

Susan's bird encounters didn't stop there but continued when she took her usual Sunday morning walk around a local lake. The huge lake, fringed with weeping willows and set in a park, is a favorite spot for fishing, boating and picnics. Susan never participated in any of these activities, preferring a good walk once a week to offset her sedentary office life, and she had followed this same routine for many years. Halfway through her walk on this particular Sunday, she heard a cacophony coming from somewhere above her, and when she looked up she saw three crows in a tree peering down at her, all chattering at once as if trying to attract her attention. She didn't take much notice, but as she continued with her walk, the squawking sounds never left her. She soon realized the crows were actually following her around the lake, flying from tree to tree; every time she stopped, the crows stopped and squawked at her, and when she moved away the crows tagged along. Susan looked around and didn't see anybody else near her, and couldn't understand why the crows were targeting her in particular. If this wasn't enough to unnerve her, she looked away from the crows just in time to see a dove flying straight towards her, which then proceeded to circle around her a few times at chest height, before flying off at the same time as the crows. This was the point at which she ran all the way back to her car, any residual pain in her back completely forgotten.

At her next session Susan was reluctant to tell me about the birds, in case I thought she was making it all up. When she eventually related the weekend's events I was fascinated, and as I jotted the information down in my notes, I got a strong feeling there was something very significant for both of us to understand. She asked me why the birds had acted so out of character, but at that stage all I could tell her was it seemed the birds were trying to give her some sort of message, but I didn't know what. It was clear the birds Susan encountered that weekend were trying to make some sort of contact by making themselves obvious, either in the dream state or physically. I wondered what it meant and, more importantly, what the birds were trying to tell her; their erratic behavior seemed more than just a quirk of nature.

A few days later I discussed the matter with a lady called Jackie Te Braake, a spiritual teacher in South Africa, and told her I thought the birds were trying to communicate with my patient. She confirmed my suspicions and then went on to explain that all birds are spiritual communicators, each one bringing its own specific message. I was astonished because I had never before looked upon birds in this way, and it was as if a light had been switched on in my head. I was even more awestruck when Jackie told me the specific meaning of each of Susan's birds: sunbirds represented JOY AND HAPPINESS, plovers represented GUIDANCE, owls represented WISDOM, crows represented CHANGE, and doves represented PEACE.

Susan had experienced an emotionally traumatic incident five years previously but she had refused to deal with it because it was too painful; as a result, she had pushed it to the back of her mind. The repressed root fears stemmed from her childhood, but the stubborn reluctance to bring all the memories to the surface and process them, meant she was stopping herself from forgiving and moving forward in life to new and more enriching experiences.

With that in mind, the messages the birds were trying to convey to Susan became clear: she would find joy and happiness (sunbird) in her life once she made the wise decision (owl) to deal effectively with the fears and negative beliefs that were holding her back; her soul, in its wisdom (owl), was telling her it was now time she forgave the necessary people and herself because this was the only way she would ever create positive changes (crow) in her life. Peace of mind (dove) would not only come from the closure of that chapter in her life, but also from the knowledge that she was not alone and was always being guided (plover) from higher realms.

The number three (three owls and three crows) was uncannily significant because Susan had three main fears she clung to in life – a fear of rejection, a fear of not being able to stand up for herself, and a fear of not being worthy of anything good in her life. There was a lot of inner work in store for Susan: she first had to acknowledge her fears, and then she had to go back to her childhood to see what precipitated these fears in the first place so that she could see them for what they truly were – illusions built around a child's perception of the way things were. This would eventually bring her into a space of forgiveness, and enable her to release these negative beliefs that kept her chained to her past. The birds had come into Susan's life at a time when it was imperative for her to deal with her fears and negative beliefs that were stopping her from moving forward in life. Her physical symptoms were also an indication that these issues needed to be addressed, but as she chose to ignore these signs, Heaven sent the birds, its divine messengers, to reinforce the message.

Birds had given me great enjoyment in many, many ways throughout my life, but this new awareness that birds are spiritual communicators and divine emissaries, suddenly cast them in a whole new light. I felt both excited and humbled with this new knowledge. I wanted to know more so I could understand and learn the language of birds. As I delved deeper, I began to realize that not only did each bird hold a symbolic key word, a message of inspiration and guidance, but also everything about birds is symbolic and archetypal in nature. Birds are always around us, audibly and visually enriching our lives by their presence, but it is *when they act out of character* that one has to sit up and take note, because this is the time they are giving us their message. It wasn't long before I was intuitively receiving the message each bird embraced.

A few months after Susan's experience, another incident took place involving a bird, but this time it happened to me. It was as if the heavens were trying to make sure I was grasping the whole concept of the symbology of birds, and also grasping that it wasn't just in my imagination or a chance happening when Nature missed a beat.

For about a year I was plagued with a strong nagging feeling I had to visit the United States of America. I had no idea why, because I had never been to the States before and didn't know anybody there. Eventually, the urge became so strong that I could not ignore it any longer, so I drew up an itinerary and booked a ticket via London so I could visit my parents at the same time. My parents were used to my doing things on a whim, and on these occasions I never tried to offer an explanation because half the time I didn't know myself why I was doing the things I did – I just *knew* I had to do them.

I stayed in America for a month and fell in love with the country. I enjoyed my time there and felt very at home, and it was great learning about the different birds (different to me) outside my hotel window, like blue jays and cardinals. But in spite of the wonderful holiday, I still do not know why my angels had insisted I visited America, because nothing tangible happened there, in the physical sense, to justify the trip. Yet I know in my heart that I did the right thing by going, and I did come away feeling different inside, as if I were walking around in a new energy field.

Two weeks before I left for my overseas trip I was watering the garden early one evening when a bird suddenly flew straight at me, causing me to dive out of the way to avoid a collision. All I caught sight of was the bird's speckled chest, and I remember thinking to myself, "He obviously hasn't got his pilot's license yet". A little while later, as I stood next to a tree, I became aware of the same bird sitting on a branch in front of me, so close I could have reached out and touched it. It was a young red-chested cuckoo. For the next week, the cuckoo made a concerted effort to make sure it was seen by strategically placing itself where I couldn't miss it – on the roof of my car, on the outside lounge windowsill, in a nearby tree, on the roof of the house, and one day it even flew into the house and sat on my sofa!

I had often heard cuckoos as they flew over my neighbourhood, but they are not suburban birds, and are rarely found sitting in a garden, let alone a sofa. The cuckoo, like Susan's birds, acted in ways that were totally out of character, and by this very fact I knew there was a message for me.

The message of a cuckoo is TRUST. I went to America on a "gut feel", and what I had hoped would happen and what I expected from the trip didn't materialize. I was being told via the cuckoo to *trust* my intuition, and to *trust* there was a higher reason for my journey, even if it didn't make any sense to my logical brain. I must admit there were a few times after I got back when I wondered whether I had wasted my money taking this trip, money that could have been spent on wiser projects at home, such as having my car serviced or the house painted. But every time these thoughts entered my mind, I remembered the little cuckoo and its message, and even though I still don't know why the trip had to happen, I trust that it was meant to be.

In my quest to learn more about the symbology of birds and the messages they brought, I began asking friends, family and patients for any stories they might have regarding unusual behavior of birds, and I was inundated with lovely tales. By far the commonest theme was a departed loved one (usually a parent) coming back as a bird. I would hear things like, "Ever since my father died there has been this particular starling who is always in my garden. I'm sure it is my father", or, "I know my mother has come back as the dove that comes to my back door the same time every day".

I remember being away at a sports training camp when I was a teenager, where one of the mothers, Jean, who had volunteered to help look after the team, would tell us stories every night in the dormitory. One story that stuck in my mind was that just before Jean's mother died, the old lady promised Jean that she would always be around and never leave her. Jean said that a few months after her mother passed away, a blackbird started to sit on her kitchen windowsill every day, gently tapping the glass to get her attention. This daily routine went on for years, and Jean was convinced the blackbird was her mother keeping her promise to always be near her. The message of a European blackbird (a thrush) is NURTURING AND CARING, and it represents the Mother archetype.

In Native American Indian folklore, many tribes believed that the spirit of their deceased lived on in the physical form of birds; the Powhatans believed that it was specifically the souls of their chiefs that continued living in birds and so they took great care not to harm them. In Africa it is also widely believed by many tribes that the soul of the departed takes on the form of a bird, in particular a songbird. One popular African folk story tells of a man who never appreciated his wife and often neglected her, but one day she was killed and her soul took the form of a songbird. During the day the songbird would fly back to her marital hut while her husband was at work, and after taking off her feathers she would sweep the floors, crush the corn and make food ready for when her husband returned. But just before he did, she would don her feathers and fly away. While the husband still benefitted from her labors, he missed her physical presence, but the only way he could bring her back for good was to lure her with love and appreciation. The moral of this story is, always count your blessings, for only when they are taken away from you will you realize just how blessed you were all along.

Despite the knowledge that a soul has infinite abilities, I am not convinced that a human soul would come back to the earth plane in the physical form of a bird. What I do believe, however, is that birds will act as mediators between the departed soul and the people left on earth. In the story above about Jean, her mother, after she died, used the blackbird (representing the mother figure), to act as a messenger between her and her daughter, to let her daughter know she is always around. There are a lot of people who would like the reassurance that a loved one who has passed away is not gone forever, but is still around. For many, it is difficult to comprehend that death isn't final but rather a transition into another dimension, the spirit world – our true home – and it is sometimes just as frustrating for someone in spirit to get a message through to us, to let us know they are alive and well, as it is for us wanting to hear from them. People in spirit use many means to let us know they are fine, and sending the message via the bird kingdom is just one way.

Another example of someone in spirit using a bird as a messenger can be found in Joel Rothschild's book *Signals*, a touching true-life story about two men living with full-blown AIDS in Los Angeles.[1] When one of the men takes his own life, he continues to help and guide his friend from the realm of spirit. As a result of this communication, the man left behind on earth, Joel Rothschild, finally overcomes the anger and despair of his friend leaving him, and starts using his growing psychic awareness to lovingly help others with support and encouragement. Several times throughout his book, Joel mentions that a hummingbird made its presence known, not only to him but also to other people connected with the manuscript of the book. The message of a hummingbird is FORGIVENESS. I believe that Joel's friend, Albert, through the hummingbird, was asking Joel to forgive him for taking his own life, leaving Joel feeling alone, angry, confused, and without an ally in his fight against the disease of AIDS. As Joel emotionally healed, the communication with Albert in the spirit world led to Joel's discovering psychic gifts he didn't know he possessed. Albert continued to use the hummingbird as his messenger, but as time went on, I believe it was to reinforce the message that love is the most powerful healer, and the only way to get to that true space of love is through forgiveness.

Jenny, another patient of mine, told me that for a whole month an olive thrush would come into her kitchen and stand by the backdoor while she prepared the evening meal. She said she found herself chatting to the bird, telling the thrush all about her problems and worries, and she felt a lot better for having done so. Jenny, who is an only child and now in her fifties, always had a difficult relationship with her mother, and at the time of her long talks with the thrush (mother archetype) she was going through a particularly bad patch with her mother, complaining that her mother never listened to what she had to say and was never there for her when she needed her. When Jenny really needed to talk to a mother figure, the thrush stepped in as a surrogate mother. But the thrush was also telling her that it was now time to heal the rift between herself and her mother.

Birds now held new meaning for me, and the more stories I heard, the more fascinated I became. Birds not only bring individual messages of inspiration and guidance; they bring messages from departed loved ones as well, to let us know they are still with us. But their role as spiritual communicators goes much deeper. For one thing, birds can symbolically teach us about the spiritual side of life.

Chapter Three
Link with the Divine

"The courage to heal and live life in spirit while in the flesh indicates our acceptance of our essence and magnificence."

Mmatshilo Motsei, *Hearing Visions, Seeing Voices*
South African author

Why are We Here?

Since time immemorial the uppermost questions in the human mind have been, "What is the meaning of life?" and "Why am I here?" – which have kept philosophers and other great thinkers on their toes for centuries.

According to Edgar Cayce, the renowned American psychic who gave thousands of readings while in a trance-like state in the late 19th and early 20th centuries, God created souls as an expression of Himself, for companionship, and as His co-creators, and He gave them the grace of free will. Every soul was created as a separate entity, and as each individual soul had a free will, its first thoughts, ideas and forms of expression were slightly different from the next, resulting in each soul building its own unique personality and character. At this stage, souls knew of their individuality but also that they were still one with God in spirit and in purpose. Unfortunately, many souls became so captivated by their own creative powers that they began to create according to their own will, which was not necessarily in accordance to God's will or Universal principles; as they became more materially-minded instead of spiritually-minded, a mental separation from God ensued. When souls began to inhabit the earth plane in human bodies to seek new experiences for themselves, they continued indulging in their own power of free will, forgetting about their divine expression, and succumbed to carnal temptations, materialism and greed.[1] But instead of recalling the souls back to Heaven so that they could start over, God in His wisdom decided to allow these souls to continue living on the material plane of Earth, so that they could one day learn for themselves that negativity and fear would never achieve divine harmony and unity.

The reason why we are here, then, is to heal our mental separation from God by remembering who we are – unique individuals AND divine beings. As co-creators with God, we are here to use our inherent divine energies to create the lives we have always wanted, and to help create a better world in which to live. More specifically, we are here to learn how to consciously create. We are now waking up to the fact that we create our own lives, and that we create according to our beliefs, attitudes and thoughts. In fact, it is our beliefs, attitudes and thoughts, fuelled by our emotions, that determine what choices we make in life, and ultimately what we bring into our reality. Every aspect of our lives is a reflection of our beliefs and thought patterns; those areas that are not working as well as they might, are the areas we have been creating according to negative beliefs.

In any given lifetime, each of us chooses our own set of fears and negative beliefs we wish to work on. Our spiritual journeys involve recognizing and changing our negative perceptions, and mastering the fears that hold the negative beliefs in place, so that we can create lives for ourselves that are full of love, joy and happiness. Taking conscious control of our lives means using our gift of free will to make choices and decisions that will benefit us, empower us, and will not harm anybody else in the process, rather than making choices based on unconscious fears. Taking conscious control also means being able to view our lives from a higher perspective, and seeing things *as they really are.*

William Shakespeare wrote: "All the world's a stage, and all the men and women merely players". Before we incarnated, we decided what fears and negative beliefs we wanted to work on in this life, as well as the positive beliefs we wanted to enhance. On the strength of this, and with the help of our spirit guides and angels, we then wrote a play entitled *Our Life,* based on what we wanted to do and learn, and the talents we wanted to utilize, with us in the leading role. We worked out the different scenarios, the opportunities and the experiences we needed, and all the people who would play the rest of the cast. Each of our plays is different and unique to us. For example, we may have decided that in this life we wanted to work on our fears of financial insecurity and so we might begin our play with us being born into poverty, or we may have decided to put the lesson further on in the play, and just when we think we are financially secure, we lose our jobs and are prompted to look at what creative talents we have that we can use to make money. Or we may have decided we want to work on forgiveness and so we chose someone to betray us; or we want to work on intimate relationships and decide to have fighting parents who divorce.

The only problem is that, as soon as we are born, we have no conscious recollection of our play or even of our writing it. Our soul knows the plot, but we do not. Then, as our lives unfold according to the script, we start to complain about the lack of money, the lack of love, failed relationships, the lack of success, poor health, and so on. If this isn't enough, we then look around to find someone to accuse for the mess we find ourselves in, and we start to blame our parents, our siblings, our schoolteachers, our bosses, or our mates. But these people are part of the cast and are acting out the script of our play EXACTLY AS WE WROTE IT. Or we blame God for the life we've got, and yet He gave us the thumbs-up to go ahead to produce our play on earth, and is overseeing every part of it.

It would help if we could occasionally watch our own play as an objective member of the audience. Then we would be able to see from an impersonal perspective the true role of every actor and how very important each one's part is to the plot. As each scene moved onto the next, it wouldn't be long before we would know the underlying attitudes, beliefs and thoughts held by the person in the starring role (us), which were influencing the choices and decisions being made, as they would be a common theme running throughout the play.

When we wrote our play, the one thing we did do was to leave the ending blank, because we knew that we have a will and the power of choice. How willing we are to learn and change, and to what extent, determines the outcome of the play. When one lifetime play comes to the end it is not the finale, however, because our souls are always spiritually growing. Each play is just a part of an eternally-running serial.

Once we understand that everything that happens to us in life, and everybody who has ever been a part of our lives, was lovingly chosen *by* us to help us with our life lessons, perhaps we will stop taking life so seriously and so personally, and start having fun. There is a spiritual law that says no one is allowed to do anything to us without our having given him or her our permission first, whether this was an arrangement before we incarnated, or whether we attracted it to ourselves by a particular belief pattern.

All God has ever asked of us, as co-creators, is that we create happy, joyous, prosperous and healthy lives for ourselves, because when we are able to do this, we are creating according to Divine principles and wisdom. And to make our spiritual journeys easier, God has provided a wealth of support and guidance from all realms, which are freely accessible to everyone. Birds are one part of this spiritual support system.

Spirit Guides

People have often asked me about the difference between angels and spirit guides, for certainly the terms have been used interchangeably, which has led to the confusion. Quite honestly, it is not important which term we use, or to whom we attribute any help or guidance, as long as we realize that there is always help coming from the spiritual realms.

As a general guideline, all of us have *two* principal spirit guides, a male and a female, that are with us throughout the whole of our incarnation, and who literally never leave our sides. The two have equal roles in our lives, though most people will be more aware of one than of the other. They are not the male and female aspects of one being; they are two separate beings. Those who have seen their spirit guides will notice that they usually appear in human form, and in a guise to which we can easily relate. A guide that appears as a Native American Indian chief or Egyptian Priestess is no more spiritually advanced than one that appears as a kindly old Victorian gentleman. It is just a way for us to perceive them. These two guides are our best friends, there to advise us, to counsel us, to encourage us, and to be with us every step of the way. But they will never take away our responsibilities.

From the time I started reading spiritual books in childhood, I was led to believe that we have only one main spirit guide, and for many years I was very confused because I could always see two guides around me, a male and a female. In my adult years the male, John, has been more dominant and the one that does most of the talking, but when I was a child it was the female, Amelia, who appears to me as a nun, that was more evident. Nevertheless, the two of them are always there together, side by side. Now I realize that I am not unique in having two main guides, but that everyone does.

We also have a myriad of other guides that come and go depending on the support and help we need at any given time in our lives. If, for example, we are going through a crisis like a bereavement, divorce, illness or loss of job, there will be certain guides that come to help support us through this time, and once we are over the crisis they will leave again. Then we have specialist guides who help us in the career or vocation we have chosen, or in any creative pursuit we have taken up. So, along with our two main guides, we have a guide for every eventuality! Some of the guides have spent time on the earth plane experiencing life as a human being, and have first-hand knowledge of what it is like to live life on earth, with all the accompanying human emotions. These guides can include family members and friends who have passed on into the world of spirit.

Angels

In her book, *A Little Light on Angels*, Diana Cooper says that angels are high-vibrating spiritual beings, and that God "appoints angels as guides, protectors and helpers for His creation and uses them as His messengers".[2] Angels, in their role as divine messengers, have brought hope, guidance, warnings, wisdom, and comfort to humanity throughout the ages. They are featured in many religious texts, and in African mythology angels are thought of as pure light, created by God to help mortals to become more virtuous, and they are said to be able to appear in any shape or form.

Cooper says there are different types of angels, classified according to their level of advancement and their place on the angelic scale of hierarchy. At the very top are the Seraphims, Cherubims, and Thrones, then come the Dominions, Virtues, and Powers, and finally the Principalities, Archangels and angels. She points out that angels are on their own evolutionary path and of a different vibration, but they have been known to assume the guise of a human when helping someone in need. Angels are guardians and protectors of all of God's creation, from the planets and stars to whole nations and cities, humanity and all aspects of nature, and they also act as messengers between God and humans. Each of us on earth is assigned a guardian angel, a personal protector, who is with us throughout our life; we also have access to all angels and archangels, whom we can call on for assistance at any time.[3] Angels are traditionally seen to possess wings.

A friend who came to visit not long ago was telling me about the dinner party she had attended the night before. She said that the conversation had got around to a discussion of whether spirit guides and angels really existed, and one gentleman in particular had emphatically stated that they didn't exist. My friend was feeling a little confused because some of the arguments he had put forward sounded fairly plausible to her. When she asked for my opinion, I said I couldn't make up her mind for her and that she had to believe in what "felt right" for her. I then said that maybe she should pray for guidance on the matter, and as soon as those words left my lips, a robin flew into the house, startling both of us. When I told my friend that the message of a robin is PROTECTION, she smiled and said that here was her confirmation because the uncanny timing of the robin's appearance was telling her that there is always protection and guidance from higher realms, and never to doubt it.

With such wonderful support and protection from angels and spirit guides, there is no excuse for any of us to ever feel alone and frightened in this world.

The Angelic Realm

After the creation of the earth, came the creation of the mineral, plant and animal kingdoms. As each kingdom evolved it became reliant on the kingdom that went before: the mineral kingdom gives sustenance and life to the plant kingdom, and in turn the plant kingdom gives sustenance and life to the animal kingdom. The animal kingdom is reliant on the other two kingdoms for survival, and humans are dependent upon all three. Although humans differ from the other kingdoms because of their free will, no kingdom is more important than the other, and all must co-exist in harmony in order to survive.

Nature spirits and elementals such as pixies, elves, gnomes and fairies, are part of the angelic realm, though they share the earth with us. They are the guardians of the natural world, and one of their tasks is to help humanity understand how to live in harmony with all aspects of nature. The most commonly known elementals and nature spirits are the Gnomes who are the spirits of the earth, the Sylphs who are the spirits of the air, the Salamanders who are the spirits of fire, the Undines who are the spirits of water, the Fauns who are the spirits of animal life, and the Dryads who are the spirits of vegetation.

Unfortunately, as time has gone on, humans have forgotten about these little workers from the angelic realm, and have relegated them to figments of the imagination and stuff of children's fairytales. A remarkable example of what can be achieved when consciously working with the nature spirits and elementals, was demonstrated at the Findhorn Foundation, a spiritual center in the north of Scotland. A woman called Dorothy Maclean, one of the co-founders of the Findhorn Foundation, had a tremendous affinity and rapport with nature spirits. She joined Eileen and Peter Caddy, the other co-founders, at a caravan park on a barren piece of land just outside the village of

Forres, where Eileen was spiritually guided to set up home with her husband. Once there, they were instructed by spirit to start a garden, but the harsh environment and sandy ground were not conducive to growing much of anything. But, inspired and led by the nature spirits, who taught them how to work in harmony with nature, they achieved the seemingly impossible, and for seven years they not only managed to grow healthy flowers and vegetables, but to grow them in ridiculously large sizes. Word got around, and gradually a community began to form around the caravan park. Under Eileen's guidance, the Findhorn Foundation has continued to develop and is now world-renowned as a leading center for spiritual development.

The Link Between Birds and Angelic Beings

Throughout the ages birds have been seen as messengers of gods, as angels, as teachers, and even as gods themselves. Angels and birds both possess wings, and birds are the only members of the animal kingdom that can sing, while angels are the only spiritual beings that sing in the heavenly choir.

It has already been mentioned that there is a hierarchy among angels, where the order depends on each one's level of advancement. Every angel has a very important role to play as a protector and a helper of God, but the responsibilities that go with each role differ according to where they are on the scale of their evolution. This can range from an angel in the higher realms being responsible for protecting the whole Universe, to an angel in the lower realms being responsible for protecting a single plant. Like us, angels are also evolving and growing.

The well-known Tibetan spirit, Djwhal Khul, who channeled through Alice A Bailey in the last century, explained that the bird kingdom plays an important part in the evolution of angels. He said that any angel who wishes to experience working on the earth plane as a nature spirit or elemental, has to pass through several cycles as a bird first before it can become a fairy, gnome, pixie, sylph, and so on. Also, if an angel who is advanced enough and has attained the necessary skills, wishes to pass into the human kingdom, one of the routes it can choose to take is by way of the bird kingdom, where again many cycles as a bird are undertaken. In both cases, the bird kingdom is a bridge between the spiritual angelic realm and the earth plane. The reason that birds are chosen to make the transition easier, is that angels can learn to adjust to a more solid physical form while still having the freedom to fly, which is familiar to them.[4]

When I read this, it confirmed for me what I was already beginning to suspect – namely, that BIRDS REALLY ARE ANGELS!

Djwhal Khul also said that angels in the spirit realm use birds to convey messages to us.[5]

A woman sent me a letter in which she included an interesting excerpt from Vicky Wall's book, *The Miracle of Colour Healing*. Wall, the pioneer of the color therapy called Aura-Soma, was able to see auras around all living things. In the excerpt, Vicky Wall said that one day she was watching a huge flock of starlings in her garden, and while she was admiring their sparkling blue/green auras, she noticed one starling sitting apart from the others, whose aura was different: it had a golden streak running through it. As she continued to watch, she realized this starling was the leader, for he eventually banded the rest of the flock together, and flew off with the other starlings in tow. After this, she took note of any bird that had a gold streak through its aura, and found that it was always the leader of the flock.[6] It could be that the bird who is the leader, the one with the golden streak through its aura, is the angel who is coming to the end of its many cycles as a bird and, therefore, being more advanced, it takes the role of leading the less experienced birds in the flock.

Another link between birds and angels can be found in Diana Cooper's *Angel Inspiration*, where she says that angels use little white feathers as a way of drawing our attention to them. She says that whenever we find a little white feather, it is informing us that an angel is present, and we must be mindful of what we are thinking about at the time we come across the white feather, because the angel is blessing the thought.[7] A few years ago, the husband of an elderly friend of mine was called away overseas on personal business. The first night after her husband left, this friend prayed to be watched over because she was nervous about being alone in the house, and was worried that she might have a fall and there would be nobody around to help. The following morning she noticed a little white feather lying on the carpet in the lounge next to her chair. The feather stayed next to her chair for the whole month her husband was away, and she somehow felt comforted by its presence, and even gave it a nickname. The very day her husband arrived back, the feather disappeared and she never saw it again. When this friend told me the story, I asked her whether she was aware that a white feather is the calling card of an angel. She said she wasn't, but that now she realizes her prayers had been answered that first night, and that God had sent an angel to watch over her.

The Symbolic Link Between Birds and the Soul

With their unique ability to fly, birds are not bound to the earth but can rise to the skies. This is why ancient cultures believed birds were the link between heaven and earth – they could fly to the heavens where the gods resided, taking human prayers with them, and then fly back with the divine answers and other messages.

The capacity of birds to move between the earth and the sky is symbolic of the soul in many ways: (a) it represents a soul living in the realm of spirit but incarnating on the earth in a physical form, and when that life is over, moving back again into the spirit world; (b) it represents a soul's ability to move between the spirit realm and the physical body when we are asleep; (c) it represents the soul being able to rise above human fears and frailties to attain new heights of awareness; and (d) it is symbolic of the fact that the wisdom of the soul, which can be accessed through dreams, intuitive hunches and meditation, has to be grounded into physical reality so that it doesn't lead merely to "flights of fancy".

One day after a treatment session, a patient asked me whether I thought it was possible for her to be able to come back as a bird in her next life. The question took me by surprise because this patient was an extremely pragmatic woman and someone I didn't even think believed in the continuation of the soul. I responded by asking why she wanted to come back as a bird, and she said that she had always wanted to experience the feeling of flying, not in an airplane or helicopter, but free-flying. I explained to her that after physical death her soul was capable of flying wherever it wanted, and so it wasn't necessary for her to come back as a bird to experience the same sensation.

Many people have told me how they have watched a bird soar through the air across the wide-open skies, and longed to be able to do that, too. Flying represents freedom. We are fully aware that our physical bodies are not capable of free-flying, yet, on another level, we inherently know that our souls can fly. When we watch a bird soar in the air we are remembering how it feels to be free of all physical restrictions, and to fly with total abandon. The fictional hero Superman offers a classic archetypal example of the soul/bird/flying image. The hero, in his persona of Clark Kent, has to strip off the clothes he wears while leading an ordinary civilian life (representing the removal of the physical countenance), to reveal the superhero garb underneath (representing the soul); only in this state is he able to fly and perform non-human feats.

Dreams of flying are common, especially among children. From my earliest memories in the cot, right up until I was in my early thirties, I was consciously aware of my soul leaving my body every night when I was about to go to sleep. This awareness gave me as a child an inexplicable feeling of security and peace. Once lulled into the sleep state, I would often dream, like so many other children, of flying, just like Superman. I never sported wings or a cape, yet I soared over rooftops, mountains, rivers, and endless patchwork fields, and I loved every minute of it. Maybe that is one of the reasons why I have loved birds so much since a child, because I knew my soul could fly with the best of them.

Somehow, we have come to believe in our minds that any message from God has to come in a dramatic way. If we were sitting in the garden and an angel appeared in front of us, dressed in a classic white robe with shimmering golden wings, we would jolt to attention, and the whole neighbourhood would get to know about it. If a bird came and sat next to us, we would think, "Oh, how sweet", and leave it at that. But the bird is just as much an angelic presence. God doesn't have the same dramatic sense as we do; Divine guidance often comes in the subtlest of ways. But we may miss this guidance because we are looking for something profound and sensational.

Birds, as we have seen, are part of the angelic realm and, just like their traditional counterparts, are heavenly messengers that bring us words of wisdom, guidance and encouragement when we need it most.

Chapter Four
Birds in Mythology

"Science must begin with myths, and with the criticism of myths."

Sir Karl Popper (1902–94), Austrian-born
British philosopher of science

The Importance of Mythology

One of the reasons for mythological stories in any culture is to try to explain how the world came into being, how humanity originated, and the role of humans in the world. Many creation stories spoke about the sky and the earth separating, and out of the waters that surrounded the earth, the emergence of land. Humans were then either created from the union of the god that resided in the sky and the god that resided in the earth, or the god in the sky modeled humans out of earth, mud or clay, depending on which culture was telling the story. The resulting offspring were either gods or mortals, with the gods having supernatural powers and helping to run the cosmos. The names of the gods differ from culture to culture but, in essence, the tales are very similar.

The stories of how a tribe came into being, and other subsequent tales, were officially related by the storyteller of the tribe, each tale a mixture of fact and fiction, some conveying lessons or morals, all told with great embellishment. The history of the tribe was kept alive as the stories were orally passed down from generation to generation, until eventually scribes wrote them down, making them available to the rest of the world.

In addition to depicting how the world and the human race came into being, mythological stories convey something else that plays an integral part in the spiritual growth of man.

Archetypes

Even though mythologies are ancient, it has only been in comparatively recent times, through the works of people like Swiss psychologist Carl G Jung and his students, that we have begun to unravel the hidden meanings contained in many of these stories.

According to Jung, our unconscious minds contain memories of every experience we have ever had. Some of this information moved from our conscious minds into the unconscious because we deemed it irrelevant, unimportant or too painful to remember, while other information passed straight into our unconscious minds subliminally, without our being consciously aware of it.[1]

But the unconscious mind also contains memories of which we have had no prior knowledge or experience in this life. Jung pointed out that there is what he called a *collective* unconscious that contains every experience of all of humanity. It is a universal ancestral memory to which our own unconscious minds are connected; these ancient psychological patterns contained in the collective unconscious Jung called "archetypes".[2]

Because our unconscious minds are intimately connected to the collective unconscious, archetypal patterns have a profound effect on our own individual attitudes and behavior, and by understanding them we are able to see our lives in a larger perspective.[3] When we read the adventures of the mythological gods, we sense something familiar about their patterns of behavior. This is because, while the symbols and images in mythological stories are not archetypes per se, they do represent the underlying forces of the archetypal behavioral patterns that are inherent in all of us and thus mythological stories help to make us aware of these ancient psychological patterns and provide an important bridge between the unconscious and the conscious minds.

While an in-depth analysis of archetypes is beyond the scope of this book, I have mentioned them because, when I was studying and intuitively receiving the individual message each bird brings, I came to realize that there was often an archetype attached to the message. For example, the message of a thrush is *nurturing and caring*, which is linked to the *mother* archetype; the message of a falcon is *loyalty*, which is linked to the *warrior* archetype; and the message of a heron is *solitude*, which is linked to the *hermit* archetype, and so on. Birds, then, can also help us to identify and understand personal archetypal patterns and archetypal forces that are working though us.

Birds depict, in a symbolic way, many aspects contained in mythological stories. Birds are natives of both the ground and the air, which is symbolic, not only of the separation of the earth and the sky in the stories of creation, but also of the union of the god in the sky and the god in the earth to create humans, as related in many of the myths. The element of air often represents the mind, and a bird's ability to fly through the air reflects back to us the power of our own minds – our intellect, our intuition, and the power of our thoughts and prayers, as well as the fact that our minds are collectively connected, not only with each other, but with higher minds, too. Birds are also symbolic of knowledge and wisdom from higher realms filtering down into our conscious minds and becoming available for use in our lives.

Birds and Mythology

Animals and birds were on the earth long before humans arrived. Because of this, primitive humans looked upon them as having certain powers and held them in high esteem. Early humans noticed their swiftness in flying, their sure-footedness when running, their cunning hunting skills, and their ability to forage and store food, as well as their strengths and instinctive behaviors. As a result, many of the early tribes and clans took an animal or bird whose attributes they admired and wished to emulate, to be the symbol, or totem, for their tribe, relying on it to guide and protect them. Occasionally, reverence for an animal or bird was so ardent that some tribes actually believed they were direct descendants of their totem animal, even calling themselves blood brothers. Myths grew as each tribe related stories of how a particular animal or bird came to be the revered symbol of their tribe, and it became taboo to harm or eat a totem bird or animal.

Sometimes clans and tribes named themselves after an animal or bird in which they saw attributes of the god that they worshipped, and often portrayed this god with, or as, that sacred animal or bird on their artifacts. For example, Odin, the Norse god of war, death and wisdom, was believed to be the chief god of a clan that had a raven as its totem; he was portrayed with a raven on each shoulder.

Birds often feature predominantly in mythological stories. Some cultures believed the souls of gods lived on as birds, while others believed that birds carried the souls of their gods to their final resting place. Deities were transported on the backs of birds or in chariots drawn by them, and many took on the form of a bird. In Egyptian mythology, Thoth, the ancient god of wisdom and justice and a moon god, was regularly depicted with the head of an ibis; the curved shape of the ibis beak was said to symbolize the crescent moon. White swans drew the chariot of the Greek god Apollo, while the Indian god Brahma rode upon geese and was portrayed seated on a swan. Zeus, the principal god in Greek mythology, took the form of an eagle when a more aggressive, dominant, male role was needed, but took on the form of a more passive bird, like a cuckoo or swan, when a gentler approach was needed to pursue an attractive woman.

Many North American Indian tribes believed birds created the wind and the clouds. The Dakota Indians worshipped a deity called Waukheon, or thunderbird, that was said to create the thunder and lightning by the flapping of its wings and the flashing of its eyes. In Europe the thunderbird is associated with the woodpecker; in Africa, with the hammerkop bird.

According to the channeled work of Drunvalo Melchizedek, there are five different levels of human consciousness possible on the Earth. Each level is an expansion of the one that goes before, and with each new level comes a different perspective and understanding of Life. We are presently sitting at the second level of consciousness, but we are moving into the third. (These are levels of *consciousness,* not dimensions.) This third level of consciousness is commonly called the Christ consciousness, the consciousness of unity, where we know without a shadow of doubt that we are one with each other and one with God. Melchizedek says that many ancient cultures depicted the first three levels of consciousness (the other two levels are beyond us at this stage), as animals on their artifacts. They chose an animal that lives underground to represent the first level of consciousness, an animal that lives on the ground to represent the second level, and one that flies above the ground to represent the third level. So, for example, ancient Peruvians used the rattlesnake, puma, and condor; Native American Indians used a rattlesnake, mountain lion and eagle; and Tibetans used a snake, pig and chicken – to denote the levels of consciousness from one to three, respectively.[4]

Bird-serpent Symbology

The strange association of a bird with a serpent is found in many cultures around the world, either in their mythological stories or on their artifacts. A Minoan statuette of the Snake Goddess, a mother goddess in ancient Crete, shows her holding a snake in each hand and with a bird on her head. The vulture-headed goddess Nekhebet protected Upper Egypt and her sister, the cobra-headed goddess Uadjit, protected Lower Egypt. There are also many stories of winged serpents, like dragons, and of feathered serpents, like the Aztec god Quetzalcoatl.

According to Jungians Marie-Louise von Franz and Joseph L Henderson, animals in myths and folklore often represent our primal instinctive nature,[5] whereas birds represent our spiritual aspirations.[6] So it could be said that a snake represents the earth's wisdom and the physical forces of nature, while a bird represents spiritual wisdom and the spiritual forces of nature, and the combination of the two would therefore symbolize that we are spiritual beings living in human bodies on the physical plane.

Joseph L Henderson further says that both snakes and birds symbolize transcendence,[7] a shift to new levels of awareness. Eastern philosophies have taught us that in the human body there is a latent energy that lies in a coil at the base of the spine, known as the "coiled serpent" or kundalini. Simply put, this energy gradually moves up the spine as we spiritually evolve, awakening the seven major energy centers (chakras) as it moves, and when it finally bursts through the crown of the head, true spiritual enlightenment is achieved. A little more specifically, the kundalini rises up the spine along the three-fold nervous system to the pineal gland, a small gland situated deep in the brain towards the back of the skull. Activation of the pineal gland opens the "third eye" and opens us to expanded spiritual consciousness. The bird/serpent symbology represents the rising of the kundalini (snake), spiralling upwards along the spine as we become spiritually awakened (bird); when the snake and bird finally merge (winged serpent), true enlightenment is attained as we are in total balance, total harmony, one with the Divine in mind and purpose. A symbol of the kundalini is often seen in the medical symbol of the caduceus, two snakes entwined around a winged staff.

The Tree of Life is also a symbol of the spiritual nature of physical man, and of the kundalini rising through spiritual awakening. It is often portrayed as a physical tree with roots deep into the earth, a snake curling up the trunk, and a bird sitting on top of the tree. The tree is laden with fruit to symbolize the "fruits" of spiritual enlightenment. I can't help wondering whether our Western tradition of a Christmas tree is not a reflection of the Tree of Life, because we traditionally decorate the tree with tinsel entwined around its branches like a snake, hang baubles that resemble fruit, and put a winged angel on top.

Fighting the Dragon

If winged serpents epitomize spiritual enlightenment after the snake and bird have merged as one, then how is it that we have stories of people like Saint George who went around slaying dragons. One reason could be that Satan was often portrayed as a hideous winged creature and was known as the Dragon of Dawn; in fact, in the Biblical book of Revelation, we read, "...the dragon, that old serpent, which is the Devil, and Satan..." (Rev.20:2). The Archangel Michael (the precursor of Saint George) was often depicted with sword and shield in hand, too; like Saint George, Michael represented the Knight archetype as he regularly fought and overpowered Satan (dragon).

In England, there is an order of knighthood called "The Most Distinguished Order of St. Michael and St. George", usually bestowed on those who have served the crown overseas in the Commonwealth countries. The badge has a white cross with a picture of Saint Michael (Archangel Michael) defeating Satan on one side, and Saint George and a dragon on the reverse side. The inscribed motto is *auspicium melioris aevi*, or "augury of a better age" – in other words, a sign of better things to come.

Fighting dragons was therefore synonymous to fighting evil and sin. It could be said that Satan represents our shadow side, our fears and negative beliefs, and thus "slaying the dragon" would mean mastering these fears and limiting beliefs in order to spiritually grow.

Another reason for the term "overpowering the dragon" may come from ancient times when people were aware of the fact that the Earth's energies flow along special pathways in the earth called ley lines or dragon paths. These ancient peoples built little hills or mounds at certain focal points where the earth's energies are the strongest, and these points were known as Dragon Power. Later in the Middle Ages when the Christian Church wanted to stop the pagans from worshipping their own deities in Britain and Europe, it built temples dedicated to the Archangel Michael on these mounts, later known as "Michael's Mounts". The Archangel Michael's temple built on a dragon power mount could be symbolically interpreted as "Michael overcoming the dragon".

Specific Birds in Mythology

Peacock

In Greek mythology, the goddess Hera, very powerful in her own right, became Queen of the Heavens through her marriage to Zeus. Zeus didn't stop his philandering after the marriage, and one story tells how he fell in love with a mortal woman called Niobe. When Hera found out, Zeus quickly turned Niobe into a white heifer, but Hera asked Zeus to give her the heifer as a present, which he reluctantly did. Hera immediately entrusted the heifer to Argus, a giant with a hundred eyes, to look after, but Zeus sent Hermes to kill the giant, wooing the giant to sleep with his flute and chopping off his head. In gratitude to Argus for his loyalty, Hera took his hundred eyes and scattered them over the plumage of her favorite bird, the peacock.

In China and Japan, peacocks were kept as a symbol of status and wealth, and in early Christianity, the "eyes" on the tail fan of a peacock were said to be representative of the all-seeing eye of God. In Sufi mythology, it was said that the Creator was a peacock. The story goes that one day, when the Creator saw his beauty reflected in the Mirror of Divine Essence, he was so overcome with excitement that beads of sweat broke out all over his feathers, from which humanity was created.

The message of a peacock is HONESTY. When the male peacock opens up his train of feathers to display a beautiful fan, this symbolizes how one's character should be, open and honest, never hiding the truth, especially from oneself. In the Greek mythological story above, Hera, with the peacock as her sacred bird, represented the archetype of the jealous wife, but she was up against an untrustworthy and deceitful husband; one could be facetious and say she was only trying to make an honest man of him.

Swan

The swan is featured in many mythological stories. The Navajo American Indians believed that a swan sat at each of the four corners of the world and brought the winds from these compass points, while the Sioux believed the swan to be a sacred representation of the Great Spirit. The white swan with its gracefulness was often taken as the image of femininity, in particular of virgin maidens, and in early Christianity swan ornaments were very popular as the swan's pure whiteness was said to depict Christ's attributes of purity and chastity. The common white swan is mute, except for occasional hissing noises, but it is said to utter a call when it is dying, giving rise to the phrase "swan song" to mark the final days of something or someone.

The message of a swan is TRANSFORMATION, a change in form, substance or character. This is not to be confused with the crow's archetypal meaning of shapeshifting. Shapeshifting involves a *temporary* shift into a different persona, then changing back again; transformation, on the other hand, is a life-altering change that is usually more permanent, a metamorphosis. In her book *Beyond Prophecies and Predictions,* Moira Timms states that in Hindu mythology the swan is seen to represent an elevated state of spiritual awareness, and the title of "Paramahansa", meaning Supreme Swan, is given to those who have achieved this state, as did the great spiritual teacher Paramahansa Yogananda.[8] Transformation is also beautifully illustrated in Hans Christian Andersen's story of The Ugly Duckling, where a cygnet finds itself misplaced with a family of ducks, and is shunned by its surrogate duckling siblings for being ugly with its grayish-brown plumage. One day, however, he grows (transforms) into a beautiful swan and becomes the envy of all the ducks.

The Navajo belief that four swans bring the winds is also symbolic of transformation, as winds bring changes, like the seasons. Wind, as the element of air or mind, is a reminder that changing one's mental beliefs and perceptions can certainly lead to transformation in one's life. An example of transformation on a grand scale is also illustrated in Moira Timms' *Beyond Prophecies and Predictions,* where she says that, astrologically speaking, a Golden Age in which "civilization...attains its highest peak" occurs every 25,826 years. It is an age in which people have attained the "Christ consciousness", living in total harmony with each other, with nature, and in accordance with divine laws. When the last Golden Age drifted to a close, the pole star shifted to Cygnus, The Swan, marking the transformation of humanity's gradual decline away from divine consciousness, and the start of a very long period of discord, conflict and strife.[9] The good news is that, as life is cyclical, we are well on our way towards the next Golden Age.

Falcon

A story in Egyptian mythology tells how Osiris was killed by his jealous brother Set, who made sure Osiris couldn't be brought back to life, by cutting him up into fourteen pieces and scattering the parts throughout the lands. Osiris' wife Isis went in search of the pieces of her husband, and found all except his phallus, which Thoth found and restored to enable Isis to conceive a son, Horus. Horus was brought up secretly, but when he was old enough, he vowed to avenge his father's death. In a battle with his uncle Set, Horus lost an eye to Set, but the gods stepped in and declared Horus the winner of the battle and demanded that Set give Horus back his eye. On the return of his eye, Horus gave it to his father, Osiris, which successfully resurrected him so that he could become the god of the dead. In this story, Isis represents the archetype of the mourning wife, and Horus the archetype of the faithful and loyal son.

In *The Ancient Secret of the Flower of Life,* Drunvalo Melchizedek points out that this story of Osiris symbolizes three of the five levels of consciousness on Earth. Osiris begins his life as a mortal, representing the first level of consciousness, but when he is cut up and his parts scattered around the world, his fragmented Self represents where humans are today, at the second level of consciousness. As soon as his parts are found and assembled together, he is brought back to life and resurrected into the third level of consciousness – the consciousness of unity.[10]

Horus, the god of the sky, was regarded as the protector of the royal house of Osiris and Isis, and the subsequent rulers of Egypt, the Pharaohs, were each believed to be the embodiment of Horus. Portrayed with the head of a falcon, Horus was said to have the sun and the moon as his eyes, which enabled him to see everything at the same time.

The message of a falcon is LOYALTY and its archetype is that of the Warrior. In British monarchic history, it was traditional for the crown prince to join the King's armies and lead them into battle against invaders that threatened the crown and the royal lands. This was a way of showing his loyalty and allegiance to the King, and to prove his worthiness of being the next ruler of the land he protected. He was known as the warrior prince, and in a sense, reflected the role of Horus as the dutiful son and protector of the monarchy.

Falconry, a hunting sport that originated in the Orient and was brought to England and Europe by merchants, became popular among the privileged classes. The sport involves training falcons (or hawks) to kill selected quarries like pheasants, herons and partridges. The quarries are flushed from the ground and into the air by the falconer and his dog; in the air the falcon kills them by swooping down and piercing a vital organ. The sport, in effect, is a re-enactment of the role of the warrior (falcon) who shows his loyalty to his master by defending the land from invaders (quarries).

We also find in British history that, in 1405, King Henry IV gave Sir John Stanley ownership of the Isle of Man, a small island off the northwest coast of Great Britain. In return, Sir John and all subsequent Lords of Man were required to give King Henry and every future king of England, on his Coronation Day, two falcons as a symbol of their loyalty to the crown – a tradition that was maintained until 1822 and the coronation of George IV, when the crown resumed ownership of the island. Later, when Anne Boleyn, the second wife of King Henry VIII of England, could only produce a daughter (who later became Elizabeth I) and not a son, Henry VIII grew tired of her; looking for any excuse to be rid of his wife, he accused Anne of being disloyal to him and ordered her execution. Portrayed on her badge are a crowned falcon and the Tudor rose.

Hawk

The hawk was often associated with the sun gods, or seen as a messenger of the gods because of its swiftness in flight. The Egyptian sun god Ra was often portrayed with the head of a hawk, and in Greek mythology Apollo used a hawk as his messenger. The Aztecs also saw it as a messenger, and the Egyptians used it as their symbol of wind in hieroglyphics. The Chinese saw the hawk as a bird of war, the Celts saw it as a malevolent bird, the Polynesians saw it as a prophetic bird that brought healing, and to the Hindus it was a bird that brought soma, a drink promising immortality. In Norse mythology, Freyja, wife of Odin and the moon goddess of love and fertility, was said to be a priestess of a clan that had the hawk as its totem.

The message of a hawk is VIGILENCE, and the sun gods could certainly keep a watchful eye and observe the lands from their place in the sky. To be vigilant is to be "Argus-eyed", a colloquial expression referring to the hundred-eyed giant of Greek mythology.

A lovely Hindu tale tells of how the gods wanted to test the goodness of the Indian emperor Shibi. The gods sent to Shibi's palace Agni, the god of fire, in the form of a dove, and Indra, the god of war and rain, in the form of a hawk. The hawk, a bird known to prey on other birds, chased the dove around the palace until the dove fell exhausted onto the emperor's lap. The hawk asked the emperor for the dove because it was his duty to kill other birds, but the emperor refused, saying it was his duty to protect his subjects; so the hawk told the emperor that if he wanted to save the dove he should give him a piece of his own body instead, a piece that weighed the same as the dove. The emperor cut off a piece of his leg which was weighed on scales against the dove, but it wasn't enough; he cut another piece from his leg, but the two pieces didn't match the dove's weight. The emperor continued to cut pieces off himself, but when he couldn't match the dove's weight, he threw his whole body onto the scales, and only then did this balance the scales. It was at this point that the hawk and dove revealed themselves to the emperor as the gods Agni and Indra, and congratulated him for being a worthy emperor, and for upholding the code of spiritual conduct as laid down in the Vedic scriptures. The hawk, the sign of vigilance, was an apt bird to send to observe how the emperor was going to respond to their test, while the dove was to confirm that the two gods had come in peace (the message of the dove) and had not come to harm the emperor.

Dove

As is widely recognized, the message of a dove is PEACE. In the Biblical story of the flood, it was a dove carrying an olive branch in its beak that brought proof to Noah that there was dry land and the flood had ended, signifying peace with God once more. In Christianity, the dove is a symbol of the Holy Spirit, for when John baptized Jesus, the Holy Spirit was said to have descended from heaven like a dove, and Jesus was later known as the Prince of Peace. Saints are often portrayed with a dove over their heads or on their shoulders as a symbol of the inspiration they received in their lives from the Holy Spirit. A dove was also used to symbolize the soul, and some saints were depicted with their souls leaving their bodies in the form of a dove at the time of their death. The dove is also a symbol of love, particularly a pair of white doves, and the dove was sacred to the Greek goddess of love, Aphrodite, and her Roman counterpart Venus.

The dove was the pagan symbol for the Angel of Peace, and it is also associated with many of the Mother goddesses, like the Egyptian Isis, the Babylonian Ishtar, the Phoenician Astarte, and the Virgin Mary in Christianity. Mother goddesses in mythological stories symbolically represent the archetypal patterns of the Mother, the Virgin, the Prostitute, and the Wise Woman.

In Kenya a dove is the symbol of mutual love, but for the Yoruba tribe of Nigeria, it represents prosperity and honor. It is a sacred bird for the North American Hurons and Mandans, while some North American Indians believe a dove will always lead them to water.

Eagle

North American Indians have greatly revered the eagle because of its power of flight, its beauty, and its ability to soar high in the sky, and many tribes saw it as a representation of the Great Spirit. Shamans of several cultures believed that eagles carried their souls on mystical and magical journeys, while other cultures believed that eagles carried departed souls home to the heavens. In Christianity, the evangelist John was often depicted with, or as, an eagle, and the eagle was sacred to Zeus in Greek mythology, who was often depicted with an eagle either at his feet or sitting on top of his scepter.

The message of an eagle is POWER AND STRENGTH. The eagle has been used as a sign of military and political power throughout history, and it has been the emblem of many nations that have exemplified power at some time or the other: the Roman Empire; Russia at the time of its rule over the Greek empire and Austria; Prussia; Germany when it was the Third Reich under Hitler; and the United States of America.

Moira Timms (see Swan), describes an ancient Babylonian mythological story that is not only another example of the bird/serpent symbology, but also has a slant on what is currently happening in our world today. The story goes that an eagle and a serpent made a pact to work together, whereby each would hunt for food for the other's family. But one day the eagle, who wanted the upper hand, betrayed the serpent by eating the serpent's family and offspring. Grieving, the serpent sought counsel with the sun god to ask how he could get revenge. The sun god advised him to lie in wait in a dead carcass, and when the eagle came down to feed on the carcass, the serpent could surprise him with an attack and rip off his talons and wings, which the serpent duly did.[11]

What makes this story relevant to current world affairs, according to Moira Timms, is that if a map of the stars were positioned over a map of the earth in a specific way, the constellation of Aquila (the Eagle) falls directly over the United States of America, and the constellation of Orion falls over Iran and Iraq. Orion is traditionally known as the hunter, but the name has also been translated in ancient texts as snake or serpent.[12] The ongoing battles between America (eagle) and the Middle East (serpent) are a playing out of this ancient mythological story; just as in the story, each party is trying to exert power over the other, one through domination and the other through revenge.

We saw from the bird-serpent symbology above, that the bird and the serpent are both symbols of transcendence, and are therefore equally powerful in their own right, each one with its own innate and unique forms of wisdom. The lesson today is to learn how to use that power wisely, within the parameters of divine principles. Rather than being involved in a powerful struggle to see who can gain the upper hand, it would be better for the eagle and serpent to combine the power of each one's wisdom, to become the "feathered serpent", the symbol of spiritual ascendance and maturity. As Timms beautifully puts it, "Peace cannot be achieved through power. But power can be achieved through peace."

Blue Jay

Blue Jay is a character in the creation stories of the American Indian Chinooks. He is a mischief-maker and schemer, portraying the Trickster archetype (synonymous with the Coyote of the Indians of the American southwest). One story tells how the Supernatural people bought Blue Jay's sister Ioi, as a wife, and when Blue Jay eventually found her, there was a pile of bones lying all around her that were her relatives by marriage. The bones suddenly assembled themselves into human form but, as soon as Blue Jay spoke, they fell into a crumpled heap again. Blue Jay had great fun watching the bones assemble, only to fall apart every time he spoke, and he had even greater fun mixing up the bones so that when they reassembled, they had the wrong arms, legs and heads.

The Trickster archetype reflects a childish behavior that lacks caring, responsibility and any serious purpose in life. Its message has to do with mentally growing up, and it can also be the springboard into spiritual maturity. The Roman god Mercury and his Greek counterpart Hermes are both representatives of the Trickster archetype, who have matured and are now able to take on more responsible roles – in this case, as messengers of the gods. Mercury with his winged hat and shoes and Hermes with his winged staff also reflect the bird symbology of spiritual transcendence.

The message of the Blue Jay (as with other jays) is OPPORTUNITY. The Blue Jay of mythological stories is an opportunist, grabbing every chance he can to play tricks and cause mischief. He has the juvenile mindset that he can do anything he pleases and get away with it but at the end of the day, he also has the opportunity to make the choice to grow up mentally and become a responsible adult.

Phoenix

The most well-known mythological bird is the phoenix. The stories essentially indicate that when this enigmatic bird has come to the end of its life-cycle, after about five hundred years, it builds its own funeral pyre out of wood and herbs. Ignited by the sun, flames fanned by its wings, the phoenix burns to ashes, but from the ashes a new phoenix is born to live out another life-cycle. Nobody knows exactly what type of bird the phoenix is, although it is known as a bird of great beauty. It has been described as an eagle, a heron, a pheasant, and a peacock, while others believe it isn't one particular bird but a conglomeration of all the best qualities of several birds.

The Romans used the phoenix on their coins as a sign of their invincibility and the continual might of the Roman Empire. In Chinese mythology, the phoenix represented the cardinal position of the south, the element of fire, and was associated with the yin principal of the Empress. They also believed this bird marked the place where treasure was buried.

The phoenix represents IMMORTALITY AND RESURRECTION. It indicates that energy cannot be destroyed, and that life moves in continuous cycles; it also signifies the immortality of the soul where, after "physical death", the soul lives on in other realms. In early Christianity, the phoenix symbolized the resurrection of Jesus, and in Egyptian mythology the phoenix was known as the Bennu bird and was associated with Osiris, who himself was resurrected. The triangular-shaped capstone found on top of the Egyptian pyramids is known as the Benben, named after the Benben stone, a meteorite that was said to have fallen out of the sky and kept atop a pillar in the ancient Egyptian city of Heliopolis. The stone was considered a symbol of the Bennu bird and as such represented immortality.

Mythological stories are the sacred stories of a culture, each one rich in symbolism and a story within a story. As with any tradition that is orally passed down through the generations, the storyline gets changed a little and the characters become interchangeable, depending on who tells them. But overall, these small discrepancies do not detract from the essence of the story or the message being imparted.

Chapter Five
Birds, Folklore and Superstition

A wise old owl sat in an oak;
The more he heard, the less he spoke;
The less he spoke, the more he heard.
Why aren't we all like that wise old bird?

Traditional

Folklore includes traditional stories of a community based on their customs, beliefs, and the knowledge they had at the time. Many tales were an attempt to explain the world around them and why things happened the way they did and, because they did not have the benefit of the scientific knowledge we have today, much was based on superstition.

In folklore of various cultures, birds have played many roles, from predicting the weather to predicting whom a girl is going to marry. They have followed armies to war to bring them good luck, and have been assistants to witches; some were said to have prophetic powers, while others were omens of bad luck or evil.

How Birds got their Markings

Many stories in folklore tell of how certain birds came about their particular coloring. A story in Australian aboriginal folklore tells how seven sisters were made custodians of Fire, on which they cooked and warmed themselves. They would not share this Fire with anybody, not even during the cold winter months, until a man named Wahn decided to trick the sisters. He filled a termite hill with poisonous snakes and led the unsuspecting sisters to it, as he knew termites were their favorite food. When the sisters broke open the termite hill, the snakes attacked them, and while they were busy fighting them off, Wahn stole the Fire. However, he, too, became possessive of Fire, refusing to share it with others. Eventually the people complained to the Great Spirit, who told them to take the Fire by force; He would deal with Wahn. The people stormed Wahn's Fire and took it away, and the Great Spirit turned the seven sisters into a constellation in the sky known as the Pleiades. He also cursed Wahn and turned him into a crow, as black as the logs that were charred by the Fire he had so jealously guarded.

Similarly, according to Greek mythology Apollo fell in love with Coronis and left a white crow to watch over her. Just before she was due to give birth to Apollo's child, Coronis had an affair, and the crow immediately told Apollo. The child was born and later became Asclepius, the god of medicine, but Apollo put Coronis and her lover to death and cursed the crow, causing its plumage to turn black.

The red-winged blackbird of America was said to have got the red marks on its wings when a blackbird tried to stop a wicked man from setting fire to fields. As the bird raised the alarm, the wicked man threw stones at it, hitting its wings and making them bleed.

The bluebird was said to have been an ugly gray color. After bathing four times in a sacred lake in the mountains while singing sacred songs, it lost all its feathers; when it bathed for the fifth time, its feathers turned to a beautiful blue.

There are different stories as to how the robin got its red breast. One of the popular ones tells that when the robin went in search of primeval Fire in the days when the world was dark and cold, it found the Fire and, during the long journey to bring it back to the people, leant over the Fire every night to keep it from going out. In the process, its breast became red and burnt.

Crossbills, a type of finch with mandibles that cross over at the tip, were said to have got their beaks bent when they tried to pull out the nails that pinned Jesus to his cross, and that the red on their breasts was Jesus' blood.

The Wishbone

The wishbone of a chicken has been considered lucky for centuries, possibly because it is shaped like a horseshoe. Found at the top of the breast near the neck, it has the same appeal as a Chinese fortune cookie. It works on the premise that, if two people each hold one arm of the wishbone with their little fingers, and both make a wish as they pull the wishbone apart, the person who is left holding the larger half of the bone will be granted their wish.

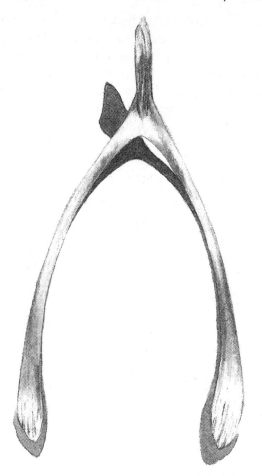

On a more practical note, chickens were often used as payment in poor rural communities when visiting the physician or healer. As part of the healing service, the wishbone was removed from a dead chicken and given to the patient to hold while prayers for healing were said for the complaint. It literally became a "wishbone". Afterwards, the wishbone was dried and hung up in the physician's window so that the patient could use the same wishbone as a prayer tool on their next visit to the physician.

Looking for Love?

The sighting of particular birds by an unmarried woman held a lot of significance as to whom and when she would marry, if at all. It was said that a young maiden could make a wish for marriage on hearing the first call of a whippoorwill, while others believed that if the whippoorwill called once the maiden would marry the man of her dreams within the year, if it called twice she would marry that man but only after a while, and if it called three or more times she wouldn't marry at all. In England and America it was said that the first bird a young lady saw on St. Valentine's Day, the 14th of February, indicated the type of man she would eventually marry: a blackbird meant she would marry a clergyman; a robin, a sailor; a yellow-colored bird, a rich man; a sparrow, a farmer; a bluebird, a happy man; a crossbill, a quarrelsome man; and a dove, a good man. If the first bird she saw was a woodpecker, she would never marry.

A friend of mine who is married to an Australian told me one day that, according to Australian aboriginal folklore, if a kookaburra is seen during a wedding ceremony, the couple will have a child soon. She said that when her son got married in Australia in an outdoor wedding, a kookaburra sat in a tree next to where her son and future wife were taking their vows, and within the year they had a baby boy.

Birds as Ill Omens

In Roman times, certain priests called augurs practiced an ancient form of divination called augury, wherein they would look for signs in nature to foretell future events. Any sign seen on their left was favorable, while any sign on the right was regarded as an ill omen. In one form of augury called ornithomancy, the priests would interpret the flight patterns and songs of birds.

Many birds are said to portend bad luck, danger, and even death by their sightings or by their behavior. In English folklore it was said that if a bird tapped on your window with its beak, it was a warning of an impending disaster, but if it actually flew into your house, it signified death for someone living in that house. If you saw a flock of birds flying from right to left it was a bad omen, and in France it was believed that the souls of children who had died without being baptized would reside eternally in birds. In Scotland, if a pet caged bird died on the day of a wedding of a family member, the marriage was doomed from the outset.

In England, the robin was thought of as being sacred because of its red breast, and it was believed that anyone harming a robin would be struck down by lightning, or at the very least that person's cow would start producing bloody milk. In Europe, human hair that had been cut was disposed of very carefully because it was said that if a bird used that hair to build its nest, the person whose hair it was would suffer with headaches for evermore, or they would suffer with boils and other skin complaints.

In nautical legends, a cormorant seen sitting on the top of a church spire predicted a shipwreck or a tragedy at sea, while an albatross spotted at sea indicated storms and bad weather ahead. Killing this bird was even worse, as it meant total disaster for the ship and its crew, as immortalized in Samuel Taylor Coleridge's poem, 'The Rime of the Ancient Mariner'.

Superstition

The above stories are steeped in superstition. Superstitions are an interpretation of why something happens according to one's beliefs, which can lead to irrational fears of what cannot be logically explained. Many common superstitions derive from a time when people didn't have scientific knowledge of how or why things happened, so their explanations were based on their beliefs and knowledge of the day. If, for example, someone lived in a farming community, and during a violent thunderstorm everybody else's barn was struck by lightning but not theirs, it could be reasoned that it was because their barn was the only one in the neighbourhood that had swallows nesting in it at the time. This rumor would spread through the community until it would be solemnly believed that lightning wouldn't strike a barn that had nesting swallows.

The fears that surround many superstitions came from people being afraid of the supernatural, and also because witchcraft and occult studies were thought of as heresy in those days, punishable by death.

Whether we care to admit it or not, all of us are superstitious about something in our lives. It might be old classics such as walking under a ladder, putting outdoor shoes on the bed, or opening an umbrella inside the house, because these actions are supposed to bring bad luck; or we might carry a lucky charm around in our purse or pocket – perhaps a rabbit's foot or a lucky coin or bead. Rituals based on superstitions are rife among sportsmen and women, musicians, and even heads of big corporations, to name a few.

Superstitions should be viewed in a lighthearted manner and in the context of being only a *perception*. We can believe in whatever we choose, but what we choose to believe will become part of our reality. And the more importance we attach to a belief, the firmer it will be embedded in our reality. In other words, what we believe will come true for us.

I have a lucky charm that is a tiny hedgehog brooch I bought at my convent school bazaar when I was five years old. Even though today his snout is crooked and most of his bristles have fallen out, rendering him nearly bald, he is ever present in my purse. But if I went on holiday and left my hedgehog brooch at home, my whole world wouldn't come to an end, nor would I believe that every natural disaster would befall me while I was away, just because I didn't have my lucky mascot with me. I love my little hedgehog and refer to him as my lucky charm, but I don't attach enough importance to him to believe that he will save me from disaster. Beliefs should never put a person in a place of fear, or lead to obsession.

One night, a friend of mine heard the hooting of an owl and rushed outside, as she had never seen or heard an owl in their neighbourhood before. As an adult she had read and heard many stories that owls were a sign of bad luck, and that night, to her horror, she found the owl sitting on the roof of her house. Two months later her husband of twenty years walked out on her unexpectedly. She is convinced that it was the owl that had been the negative influence that led to her subsequent divorce, and she has been fearful of owls ever since. This woman grew up on a remote farm where calls and sightings of wild owls were commonplace; those years, she said, were the happiest times of her life and nothing 'bad' ever happened. Her irrational fear of owls stems from her *choosing* to believe owls to be a bad omen; instead, she could have chosen to take the call of an owl to invoke beautiful and happy memories of her childhood.

Attaching importance to a belief is what folklore is all about. One culture might regard a certain bird with fear, declaring it an omen of doom and death, while another culture regards the same bird with reverence. Some African tribes, for example, fear vultures, as it is believed they bring disaster to a traveler, but other tribes look upon vultures as possessing great wisdom because they survive by eating dead carcasses.

Owls

Of all birds, the owl is probably the one with the greatest stigma attached to it, because it is associated with death in many cultures. This unfair reputation derives from the fact that the owl is nocturnal, a creature of the night, and many cultures believe that only witches and demons roam about at night. The owl's upright posture, large round head with big forward-facing eyes, noiseless flight, and haunting cries that range from a melancholic "hoo-hoo" to an eerie screech, contribute to its sinister reputation.

In Roman times the sighting of an owl was taken to spell disaster, while to hear the call of an owl meant imminent death. Legend has it that the deaths of Roman emperors Julius Caesar and Caesar Augustus were foretold by the hoot of an owl. To help keep away evil, dead owls were nailed to the front doors of houses, a practice continued in England until a couple of centuries ago.

In England it was said that the screech of a barn owl was to bode ill fortune, and in some communities it was an omen of death. Eating owl eggs was thought to be a cure for alcoholism, and owl eggs were given to children in the belief that they would be prevented from turning to drink later in life. It was also believed that if you walked around and around a tree with an owl in it, the owl would keep turning his head until he eventually wrung his own neck.

The Vedic god of death was said to use an owl to deliver his messages, the Australian aboriginals viewed the owl as the bearer of bad news, in China and Japan the owl was associated with evil spirits, and the Algonquin Native American Indians saw the owl as the helper of the Lord of the Dead.

The owl's reputation of being a "wise old bird" derives from mythologies where it was honored and revered as a symbol of wisdom. The owl was associated with the Greek goddess of wisdom Athene, who was often depicted with an owl sitting on her shoulder, where it was said the owl would reveal hidden truths to her so that the whole truth could be told to the person seeking counsel with her.

In Celtic mythology, the owl was seen to represent the archetype of the wise woman or crone. Known for its keen night vision, the owl was looked upon as a guide through the darkness. In Welsh mythology, the goddess Arianrhod often shapeshifted into an owl, where she was able to look into a person's soul with her big owl eyes. Some Native American Indian tribes see the owl as a protector of the night and hold it in reverence for its night vision, aspiring to draw to themselves this strength by honoring it.

The Berber tribes in the High Atlas Mountains of North Africa believe there is an owl that suckles human babies at its breasts, but one breast will make the baby healthy, while the other breast will make the baby ill and cause it to die. In other parts of Africa the owl is usually seen as a messenger of impending danger. The Zulu look upon owls as "policemen" that patrol the night, relying on them to watch over the tribe and to warn them of any dangers. In Botswana it is believed an owl is connected to night witches who will warn the tribe of an approaching enemy, and in Malawi, if an owl is heard to hoot, it is the job of the tribal chief to speak to the owl to ask if there is danger in the area from lurking enemies, or if witchcraft is being practiced nearby. It is said the owl always answers him.

Ravens

Birds with black plumage, like the raven and crow, have always been considered ill omens, because the color black is traditionally associated with death, evil and negativity. In England, tombstones used to be colloquially known as ravenstones.

It is interesting that the negative connotation of black derives from the fact that this color is seen as devoid of light. But the Universe started as a black void, and out of the void came light, matter and all of creation. Black in the truest sense is a symbol of "nothingness" that holds the potential for creation. It is in this vein that many Native American Indians view the raven as a sign of magic, representing the mystery of creation.

Ravens, like owls, are viewed in folklore either as ominous or as being lucky and mystical. In England and Europe the raven was a portent of death because of its black color, raucous call and scavenging nature, and it was associated with witchcraft and black magic. Conversely, the Vikings believed ravens brought good luck and they often portrayed them on banners on their ships. In Ireland, ravens were tamed and used for divination purposes, and any person who had the gift of second sight was said to have "raven's knowledge."

In Nordic mythology the god Odin was said to have kept two ravens, one on each shoulder, representing thought and memory; the ravens would whisper to him the great knowledge they had gathered from their journeys around the world. In some North American Native folklores, the raven not only represents magic and mystery but is also seen as a trickster; there are numerous stories of his pranks, including how he cheated other animals out of their food, and how he hid all the animals in a cave to try to fool God.

Alexander the Great was said to have been guided through the desert by ravens, and in the Bible, God instructed the prophet Elijah to hide near a brook where he would be fed and kept alive by ravens who would bring him bread and meat. But when Noah released a raven to find dry land after the Flood, it didn't return.

The Tower of London in England is famous for its ravens. Originally built as a fortress in the time of William the Conqueror, the Tower has, for as long as anybody can remember, been a haven for ravens, which are actually protected by a royal decree. Legend has it that when there are no longer ravens in the tower, the monarchy will fall, and on the strength of this, six ravens are permanently kept in residence, all with their wings clipped. The Royal Observatory used to be housed at the Tower of London, and it is said that Charles II became so irritated by ravens' droppings on the end of the telescope, that he ordered the ravens to be destroyed. But when told of the legend of what would happen to the monarchy if the ravens were to disappear from the tower, he changed his mind and had the Observatory moved to Greenwich. The legend is thought to have originated from Bran Fendigaid, the Welsh god of regeneration, whose name means raven. The story goes that Bran was fighting in Ireland in honor of his sister and was mortally wounded. But before he died he requested his head be cut off and buried on the White Mound, the site where the Tower of London stands today, so that he could always protect the land from this position by watching for invaders. So, in essence, it is Bran, the Raven, who must be kept at the Tower lest Britain should fall to invaders.

The negative connotations attached to some birds are based on fears and superstitions. Birds are divine messengers and, like any guide from Source, the only messages they carry are ones that will give us inspiration and empowerment. They will never convey doom and gloom, or anything else that will alarm us.

Chapter Six
How Birds have Helped Humanity

"Whatsoever we beg of God, let us also work for it."

Jeremy Taylor (1613–1667), English writer
and churchman

It is often said that a dog is man's best friend because of the unfailing devotion, loyalty and companionship a dog shows to its master. In the broader scheme of things, I think birds should be hailed as man's best friend, because they have been a constant source of inspiration to man in his quest to understand and conquer the mysteries of life.

The first bird known to have inhabited the earth was the Archaeopteryx (from the Greek words "archaios" meaning ancient and "pteryx" meaning wing), some 150 million years ago. The size of a crow, it had a long bony tail and resembled a reptile, but it was unique in that it possessed feathers and could fly. Avian evolution had begun, and as far back as eleven million years ago most of the bird families we see today were already inhabiting the earth, adapting and colonizing the four corners of the world. Once humans started to share the domain, they looked upon birds for clues on how to manage and survive life on this planet. By observing birds' behavior, humans realized, among other things, that birds could lead them to water sources, to dry land, to where food might be found – and that bird calls could warn them of approaching danger.

Birds have proven to be wonderful teachers and of great assistance to humanity in many practical matters.

Aviation

For as long as anyone can remember, humans have been enthralled by birds' ability to fly, and people have often tried to emulate flying. While some people thought that it was only the gods who were privileged to fly, either in the form of birds or by riding on a winged animal, and that flight was beyond the capacity of mere mortals, others thought differently and duly tied feathers to their arms. But no amount of vigorous flapping could get them airborne. Through trial and error, humans began to realize that flying involved a lot more than strapping on feathers or leaping off a cliff wearing a large cloak, and as time went on people started to study birds and their mechanism of flight more intently. We discovered that the shape of the wings was an important factor, as was the angle at which the wings were held, along with factors like gravity, wind speed, drag and thermals.

Around 400 BC a little-known Greek scholar called Archytas built a wooden pigeon that was able to fly, thought to be propelled by steam or gas. A hundred years later the Chinese invented kites, which were eventually made large enough to raise people off the ground, and in the 1500's Leonardo da Vinci sketched flying machines which had wings that flapped. But it was only in the 1780's that a human successfully got off the ground and into the air, in a balloon made of paper and linen, propelled by hot air generated from burning straw and wool. Other inventors elaborated on this achievement by filling the balloon with hydrogen, a gas lighter than air, and with the later addition of an engine and propellers, the airship came into being.

The British inventor who founded aerodynamics, Sir George Cayley, produced the first fixed-wing aircraft called gliders in 1804; these were successful in flight but difficult to steer. An airplane was needed that could not only hold passengers and cargo, but could be controlled in the air, and by the middle to late 1800's airplanes were being designed with engines, propellers and fixed wings. But it wasn't until 1903 that two American brothers, Orville and Wilbur Wright, built the world's first successful airplane, marking the start of a new era in aviation. Soon airplanes were being built in metal, the first transport airplane flew in 1927, De Havilland Comets became the world's first large commercial jet liner in 1952 with Boeing following in 1958, and in 1970 the world's first jumbo jet, the Boeing 747, entered the scene.

God gave birds the gift of flying and birds passed the gift on to humans. By studying birds, humans have learned how to fly and have effectively mastered the air; we now have a popular mode of transport that has made the world seem a smaller place, in easier reach of many people. Aviation has also paved the way for human space exploration and travel.

Nature's Alarm Clock and Barometer

For eons birds have acted as nature's alarm clock, notifying man and beast that a new day is about to begin and it is time to wake up. As the first rays of light pierce the eastern sky, birds from their vantage point high up in the trees joyfully herald the start of a new day with their communal singing of a dawn chorus, while from the ground the roosters crow to confirm the break of day. For civilizations that do not have the benefit of man-made clocks and watches, this has been a blessing. Waking up with the birds at sunrise and going to bed when the sun sets is still a way of life in many rural communities; the bodies of people who live this way are in sync with the natural rhythms of the earth. Unfortunately, in our modern world where the clock rules our lives, bedtime is usually dictated by our social lives or what's on television, and we rely on alarm clocks to wake us in the morning. The natural rhythms of life are long forgotten as we force our bodies to depend on artificial means to wake us up and send us to bed. Most of us are not even aware that the birds are singing as we rush around in the mornings getting ready for work and getting the children off to school. It would be much more pleasant to be woken by the gentle sounds of nature instead of the shocking clang of alarm clocks or blaring of radios.

According to "old wives' tales", when the geese are flying low in their "V" formation, or the swallows are flying low, or when the rooster crows at times other than dawn, stormy weather is on the way. But this is more than superstition, because birds are very sensitive to changes in atmospheric pressure. When storm clouds begin to mass, birds sense, like a barometer, the subsequent drop in pressure in the atmosphere, and they will respond in ways that "predict" a change in the weather. Thus they give us warning that bad weather is on its way.

The changing seasons are also highlighted by the appearance or disappearance of certain birds in a locality, due to their migratory behavior. The return of summer breeding birds, such as swifts and swallows, to a certain area, signifies that Spring has arrived; conversely, their departure marks the approach of Autumn. The first call of the cuckoo in England, the first sighting of the robin in America, the African weaver bird regaining its bright yellow plumage for the breeding season – all are indications that Spring is here.

Keeping the Ecology Balanced

Several plants produce fruit that, as it ripens, become sweet and brightly-colored, to entice fruit-eating birds. The soft fruit is easily digested and the indigestible seeds are either excreted undamaged in the droppings, or regurgitated if the seeds are large; in this way birds help to ensure the continuation and survival of these plants by spreading the seeds over a wide area. To aid this process, many fruits ripen in stages to coincide with migrant flocks' passing over. For example, in the Northern Hemisphere fruit begins to ripen in the southern parts of an area first, progressively ripening later and later as one moves further north, all timed perfectly as the fruit-eating migratory birds fly through from south to north. Hummingbirds, sunbirds and sugarbirds also play their part in the ecology by helping with pollination, unwittingly conveying pollen grains from flower to flower when feeding on the nectar.

The honeyguides of Africa are unique in that they can eat and digest wax. They help the honey badger, and sometimes humans, by showing them where to find bees' nests for their wax and honey, and once these nests are broken open, the honeyguides help themselves to a share of the spoils. Oxpeckers feed on ticks, mites and other parasites from the skin of big game animals and domestic cattle, helping to keep these animals pest-free.

While farmers consider some birds to be pests, many of the seed-eaters, insectivores and omnivores are an asset as they eat the seeds of weeds and feed on other agricultural pests like caterpillars, grasshoppers, mice and rats. Even in suburban gardens, birds like the thrush help to keep down pests by eating such garden enemies as slugs and snails. Ironically, the use of chemical pesticides to rid gardens of snails and slugs are causing a decline in the number of these birds in the garden.

Birds also provide an excellent source of organic fertilizer, called guano. The droppings of sea birds, accumulated over centuries on the islands of Peru and in West Africa, are so rich in ammonia and phosphorus that they have been marketed as a fertilizer since the 1840's.

Coal Mine Safety

The Chinese were the first to mine coal in the third century AD, but the commercial mining of coal began in England in the thirteenth century. Since those times it has been known that poisonous gases can accumulate underground in the mines which are toxic to humans and can cause devastating explosions. The main culprits were later identified as methane gas, which occurs naturally in the coal seams and can be highly explosive, and carbon monoxide, produced from the combustion of coal from blasting underground. Modern-day coal mines use air vents and large fans to circulate fresh air through the tunnels, and they are required by law to have special methane detectors to warn of any build-up of this harmful gas. In the old days of mining, however, there was no such sophisticated equipment, and the most reliable methane detector around was the humble canary. Because canaries are very sensitive to poisonous gases, a miner might carry one around in a cage with him in the mines. If the canary suddenly collapsed and died, it immediately indicated the presence of lethal amounts of methane gas. This may not have been good news for the canary, but it helped to prevent devastating explosions and subsequently saved many a miner's life. In the same way, canaries have been used on battlefields to detect the presence of toxic gases.

Carrier Pigeons

Many birds are renowned for their ability to find their way home over long distances, and humans have capitalized on this natural flair. The The Romans used to tie threads of different colors to the legs of swallows to let people at home know the result of chariot races, and both the Romans and Egyptians used pigeons to carry messages. Modern-day pigeons descend from the wild rock pigeons and were domesticated by the Egyptians as far back as 3100 BC. Pigeons have been used as a source of food, and for recreational purposes like racing, but they have always remained a firm favorite as reliable carriers of messages. The Sultan of Baghdad used pigeons to carry messages in 1150 AD, and they were used as a messenger service in Europe in the mid-19th century. Pigeons were also employed to convey messages in times of battle, from Gengis Khan who used them during his conquests, to their later use in both World War I and World War II. During World War II the National Pigeon Service was set up in England, and private breeders all over the country supplied thousands of homing pigeons to this service as part of the war effort. Although wire communication was very much in use during World Wars I and II, there were times when it wasn't safe to use this sort of communication, or the lines were down, so pigeons were dispatched with the crucial correspondence, competently delivering their messages. Pigeons are still employed by the military in many countries today.

The Theory of Evolution

British naturalist Charles Darwin became famous for his published theories on evolution, wherein he maintained that every plant and animal gradually evolved over thousands of years from a few common species, a process known as the survival of the fittest, or natural selection. He wrote a book called *The Origin of Species*, which caused an uproar at the time because his theories challenged religious belief that God created each and every species separately.

Between 1831 and 1836, Darwin went on a scientific expedition around the world on the ship HMS Beagle, serving as a naturalist. He collected specimens of fauna and flora wherever he went. At the Galapagos Islands in the Pacific Ocean, he collected, among other things, an array of what he thought were different birds from the various islands. It was only when he donated the birds to the Zoological Society of London on his return to England, that an ornithologist studied the birds and found many to be different species of the same bird, a finch, and all unique to the Galapagos. The story of the new species of finch made the newspapers the next day, and thrust Darwin's finches into the spotlight. But it was not only the finches that piqued the experts' attention, but also all the other specimens he found on the islands, including giant tortoises, iguanas, mockingbirds and a variety of plants. The excitement lay in the divergence of the different species that must nevertheless have originated and evolved from common ancestral stocks. Darwin began to realize just how important the finches and his other specimens from the Galapagos were to the theories that had been forming in his mind regarding the origin of species so, using them as his basis, he spent the rest of his life studying and writing about his theories. He even bred and cross-bred pigeons in his backyard in order to advance his studies on natural selection, to prove how the advantageous traits in a species were passed on to the next generation. The finches of the Galapagos Islands have become known as Darwin's finches; being ideal subjects because of their vast numbers, their differently-shaped beaks, and their uniqueness to the islands, they have continued to be studied over the years in a scientific quest to understand evolution.

Iridology

In the Western world alternative therapies are becoming more recognized and increasingly popular. They are not new, because most of them have been around since ancient times, but as we learn that we are energetic beings, different forms of energy healing techniques are being "rediscovered" and put to good use. The scientific art of analyzing a person's health from the iris of the eye, called iridology, has been in use since the time of Hippocrates, but the pioneer of its modern use credits a bird for its reinvention.

As a young boy growing up in Hungary, Ignaz von Peczely tried to catch an owl; in the struggle that ensued, he inadvertently broke its leg. As they continued to struggle, Peczely noticed a distinct dark line beginning to form in one of the owl's large eyes. The owl, resigned to its fate, eventually allowed itself to be caught and nursed back to health. As the weeks went by and the broken leg began to mend, Peczely noticed that, as it did so, the black line in the owl's eye gradually faded and disappeared. Peczely was fascinated, and when he later became a physician and naturopath, he started studying the irises of the eyes of his patients. To his amazement, he found that certain markings and discolorations in different zones of the iris reflected deviations from health. He began to map out these deviations and published a paper on his comparative findings. His medical colleagues shunned his unorthodox approach of diagnosing illnesses, but he persisted in his belief that the eyes held many answers to a person's health questions. Not knowing about the energy counterpart of a human body, he continued to puzzle over why inflammation would be indicated in the iris long before it manifested in the physical body. Nevertheless, his pioneering work encouraged others to continue to study and refine iridology, making it a competent diagnostic tool.

Migration

There is much about the behavior of birds we still don't understand. One enigma that continues to baffle scientists is the concept of migration. Migratory birds choose to breed in one area, and then when winter begins to set in and food becomes more scarce, they fly to another area that is completely removed from their breeding grounds, often in the opposite Hemisphere. Some bird species choose to stay near their breeding grounds if the winters are mild and only migrate if the winter is bad. Others, such as the swift, breed in Europe but as soon as autumn arrives will fly to the southern parts of Africa to wait out the European winter before flying back to Europe in the spring to breed again.

Migratory birds are able to fly very long distances, accurately finding their way between their two "homes" and often going back to their same nests year after year. In preparation for the long flights, many birds build up their fat reserves by eating vast amounts of food beforehand, with some weighing almost twice as much when they take off on their migratory flights. Many birds fly considerable distances, sometimes non-stop when flying over the sea or over barren deserts. Some species of the willow warbler, for example, weighing a mere 0.3oz, fly distances of about 8,000 miles from Alaska to winter in Africa, often flying non-stop for two days at a time.[1]

Research has shown that birds not only use landmarks like mountain ranges and rivers to find their way, but also use the position of the sun and the stars for orientation.[2] Birds also use the earth's magnetic fields as a guide, and when these magnetic fields are temporarily disrupted, for example after a significant solar flare, many birds are thrown so much off course that they arrive in places they are not usually found, to the great delight of avid bird-spotters. It has now been discovered that the pineal gland in a bird's brain contains some type of magnetic material, and scientists believe that this is the specialized sensory organ birds use to detect and navigate the earth's magnetic fields – a kind of built-in compass.[3]

Chapter Seven
Feathers

"Having opened
the door of hope
I know my spirit
will soar and
untold wonders will
be revealed."

Betty Shine, English healer, *Mind To Mind*

The Sioux Indians tell the story of Ictinke, the son of the sun god, who became tired while out walking one day and asked a passing buzzard to give him a ride on his back. The buzzard agreed, but half way through the journey, the buzzard threw Ictinke off, and Ictinke landed in a tall, hollow tree where he became stuck. Waving the raccoon tails he was wearing through a hole in the tree, Ictinke tried to get the attention of a passing tribe. Three women spotted the tails, and thinking there were raccoons stuck in the tree, made a hole, but when Ictinke jumped out, they got a fright and ran off. Ictinke then lay down on the ground and pretended to be dead; soon birds of prey began to flock around him, attracted by the raccoon tails, but when the buzzard swooped down, Ictinke leaped up and ripped off all the feathers from the buzzard's head. This is why, the Sioux say, the buzzard is bald-headed to this day.

The one distinguishing feature that makes birds unique is that they are the only members of the animal kingdom that have feathers. Feathers play a very important role and have many functions: they are light in weight to enable the bird to fly; they provide protection and insulation; and they provide the bird with color. They come in many shapes and sizes, but they basically fall into two main categories: the flight and contour feathers, and the down feathers. All contain a central shaft from which hundreds of filaments branch out, but the flight and contour feathers additionally have tiny interlocking barbs that literally zip the feather filaments together. One exception to this is on the wings of an owl, where the feathers are unzipped in order to create a softer edge like a fringe, so that the owl can fly more silently.

The flight and contour feathers are the large, strong feathers found on the outside. They are curved, firstly to create an aerodynamic surface to afford flight, and secondly to give the bird its distinctive form and appearance. The flight feathers were the feathers used for quill pens, a writing tool that has been around since Anglo Saxon times. The flight feather was chosen because it was large enough to be held in the hand and had a strong shaft that could be skillfully honed into a nib using a special knife called a pen knife. The feathers used were usually taken from a bigger bird like a goose or a swan, and it was found that for right-handed people it was better to use a feather taken from the left wing of the bird, as it was more comfortable to hold than one taken from the right wing. The opposite was true for left-handed people.[1] The word "pen" is an abbreviation of "penna", the Latin word for feather.

The down feathers, smaller, softer and fluffier, are the ones that provide most of the insulation. Birds are warm-blooded creatures whose body temperatures must be kept around 40 degrees Celsius. The down feathers work by trapping an insulating layer of air between the skin and the feathers in order to retain body heat; if birds do get cold, they fluff up their feathers to create more heat-traps of air. Down feathers from ducks or geese are often used to stuff pillows and duvets, the most notable being the eiderdown quilts which are stuffed with the down feathers of the eider duck.

Other types of feathers fall between the previous two categories, and either have a sensory function to keep the feathers arranged in order, or are bristled in texture to provide protection around the eyes and beak in particular.

Bird feathers are made of keratin, the protein that is the main constituent of human hair and nails. The feather grows out of the body from special nipple-shaped bumps called goose bumps; like our own hair and nails, once it is fully grown the feather becomes dead matter. Bird feathers are waterproof and they provide protection from ultraviolet (UV) light. Most aquatic birds produce an oily substance near the base of their tails and use their bills to smear the oil over the rest of their feathers for extra waterproofing. To oil the feathers on their heads, they rub their heads over their back feathers; chicks not old enough to produce their own oil climb through their parents' feathers to spread the oil over themselves.

Down Feather and Contour Feather

Feathers come in a range of colors. Most birds have lighter colored feathers underneath their bodies to help minimize the effect of their shadow, while some birds have feathers similar in shade to the background of their natural environment to provide natural camouflage. Females generally tend to be more drab in color than their male counterparts, so that they are less conspicuous to predators while sitting on their nests. Birds have very good eyesight, and the brightly-colored feathers and different feather patterns help each species to recognize its own members. This is not only beneficial for birds that follow one another in flight; it is also meaningful in courtship displays. The males use color, plumes and crests in their courtship displays to attract the attention of a prospective mate, and the female is able to distinguish the male from other bird species by his characteristic and distinctive markings.

Alan Fletcher, in *The Art Of Looking Sideways*, points out a very interesting fact with regard to how birds see color. He says that birds see colors in the ultraviolet spectrum, which our human eyes are unable to pick up or register. For example, we see a raven as plain and black, but to another bird the raven's plumage appears as a sparkling blue, violet and purple, and a swan that appears white to us will be seen by another bird as a "shimmering spectrum".[2] Does this reinforce the Buddha's teachings that all life is an illusion?

Birds sit on their eggs so that heat from their bodies can keep the eggs warm enough for the embryo to develop inside the shell and eventually hatch. To overcome the fact that bird feathers are great insulators, brooding birds will shed feathers from their abdomens immediately before incubation so that their bare skin, with its profusion of blood vessels, can lie against the eggs to create a more efficient heat transfer. These bald patches, known as brood patches, can be one large patch or several smaller patches, depending on how many eggs are in the nest.

The Symbology of Feathers

Although a feather is not living matter in the conventional sense, it does contain the "essence" of the bird from which it came. When a homeopath uses a pendulum to do a health analysis for someone who is not present in the same room, he or she will often use a sample of their hair as a way to connect to that person's essence, or energies, in order to find the correct remedies and dosages required. It works by the principle of the hologram, where the information of the whole is contained in each piece; a lock of hair or a bird's feather will therefore possess the whole energetic patterning and characteristics of its original owner. Scientists call it the Principle of Biological Resonance, where the organic material need not be alive but is still energetically connected and resonating with the source from which it came.[3]

Ancient civilizations knew that feathers contained the energies of the birds from which they came, and used feathers as a way to align themselves to the birds and their attributes. Similarly, feathers of birds sacred to particular gods were revered, as it was believed they provided direct access to the deities and also held important information from these gods. In the Cherokee and Dakota tribes of North America, only the warriors who had been successful in battle, and therefore had proved their might and strength in the face of adversity, were allowed to wear the feathers of an eagle. The Zuni tribe, when calling on the rain god to bring rains to the land, used four eagle feathers to represent the power of the four winds entrusted to bring the rain. In many Native American Indian tribes, the number and variety of bird feathers worn, or the way they were mounted, often showed rank in the tribe.

Shamans are traditionally seen as messengers between the different spiritual dimensions. The shamans of Siberia wear cloaks of bird feathers, not only to display the spiritual power and protection afforded them by these birds, but also as a way to symbolically help lift their souls from the material world so that they can fly in the realms of spirit. The use of feathers is apt because time is linear on the earth plane, and a bird's ability to fly through the air is symbolic of the ability to travel through time and space in order to reach other dimensions. In *Animal Speak*, Ted Andrews writes that shamans in several cultures often used prayer sticks or staffs that acted as a kind of antenna to direct the energies they were channeling. Many of these sticks were adorned with feathers, or had a bird's head carved on the top, to symbolize the power of flight into other realms.[4] It is interesting that Mary Poppins, the magical nanny in PJ Travers' book of the same name, used to fly with the aid of her umbrella that had a parrot's head carved on top of the handle.

Feathers – along with other such things as animal skins, stones, wood and bones – often became fetishes for many people of a tribe, but especially for the shaman. Fetishism comes from the Portuguese word "feitiço", meaning charm or magic; a fetish differs from an amulet, which acts as a "shield" to protect the wearer from evil. Each fetish was considered to contain a living spirit, like the nature spirit of the tree, animal or river from which it was obtained, or the spirit of a dead person, such as an ancestor. The fetish could be used for anything from self-protection to medicine, and it was the shaman who, through special incantations, instructed the spirit residing in the fetish on the role it had to play. Sometimes a fetish was thought to have magical powers, enabling the user to perform feats, like becoming invisible so he could walk in the midst of the enemy and not be seen. The type of fetish to be used was often revealed to the shaman in a dream, but whatever way a fetish came into a person's life, it was very symbolic for that person.

It was said that the Aztec god of war, Huitzilopochtli was born from a ball of feathers hidden in his mother's shirt, and he was often portrayed as a hummingbird. It was also believed that the souls of dead Aztec warriors lived on as hummingbirds. Another Aztec god, Quetzalcoatl, the son of the creator god, was depicted as a feathered serpent, sharing his name with the beautiful Quetzal bird of Guatemala and Mexico.

Down feathers provide insulation and protection for the bird, and it is symbolic that we have chosen these feathers to stuff our pillows and duvets. Being wrapped up snugly under a feathered duvet, with feather pillows under our head, gives us a feeling of warmth, security, and an inner knowing that we are protected as we lie down to sleep. There are some people who are allergic to down-feather pillows and duvets. As allergies are related to the emotions, they usually develop as a result of an unresolved emotion. Generally speaking, an allergy to down feathers can occur in people who have deep feelings of insecurity and who view the world as an unsafe place in which to live. They find it difficult to trust that there are always higher realms watching over them, and so they wrap themselves up in artificial things that give them a false sense of security, the way they wrap themselves up in duvets and pillows made of artificial fibers.

The use of color, crests and plumes by birds in their courting rituals demonstrates a spiritual law, the Law of Attraction. Our bodies are surrounded and protected by a magnetic energy field which contains all our thoughts, emotions, experiences and instincts and, like a magnet, it attracts to us everything we need in this life in order to grow spiritually. Positive beliefs will draw positive experiences to us, whereas negative beliefs will draw negative experiences. But an experience is never truly negative, because everything has the potential for soul growth. Unpleasant people or situations that we encounter in our lives are only reflecting back to us our fears, insecurities and negative beliefs that we have kept buried in our psyches, long forgotten; they are making us aware of these fears so that they can be brought to the surface and aired, enabling us to change our perceptions for the better.

We receive intuitive guidance through the right half of our brain (the female, creative, intuitive, passive side) and it is then transferred to the left side of the brain (the male, logical, rational, active side) so we can analyze the guidance and put it into action. Just as the female bird sits quietly on her eggs in the nest, so we have to be quiet and still in a brooding or meditative way, in order to hear clear guidance, or maybe to hear the answer to a prayer. Then, like chicks, once the creative ideas have hatched in our minds, we can bring in the bold male energies to put them into practice in our lives.

Newly-hatched birds grow and develop in the safety and security of the nest where they are nurtured and cared for by one or both parents, or by guardians in the case of a cuckoo or cowbird. When they are mature enough and their feathers are grown, they leave the nest and fly away to start life on their own. When our children grow up and leave home, we often use the expression, "the kids have flown the nest". Like young birds flying away from the nest in which they were raised, young human adults leave the security of the childhood home to "find their wings" and start the next phase of their lives. They must learn to take responsibility for themselves as individuals, and to find their own place in the world. "Flying the nest" may also mean, symbolically, the need to break away from traditional family beliefs, in order to be able to choose our own beliefs.

The Soul and Feathers

A feather is synonymous with the soul, metaphorically speaking. In Egyptian mythology, Ma'at was the goddess of truth, justice and the underworld, and it was her job to evaluate and judge the souls of all those who had just died. She weighed each soul against a feather; if the soul was too heavy it was sent to the underworld, but if the soul was as light as the feather it was allowed to proceed upwards to the heavens. Ma'at was often portrayed wearing an ostrich feather on her head, a symbol of truth in Egypt.

Feathers are light in weight and are the only means by which a bird is able to fly. Similarly, the soul is extremely lightweight in comparison to the dense physical body that houses it; when free from restrictions, a soul can fly uninhibited. In the same way as shamans symbolically use feathers to assist their souls to rise above the material world, feathers reflect the fact that no matter what physical obstacles are put in our way during our life's journey, we all have the capability to rise above our fears and limitations and, in so doing, we will be able to rise to new levels of understanding. If we cannot seem to get that initial lift-off, we must look at our lives to see who or what has "clipped our wings", keeping us on the ground and stopping us from attaining our goals and realizations. To rise above the negative limitations we put on ourselves, we need faith, a willing mind, and a little bit of courage – and before we know it we are soaring in the heavens.

In Greek mythology Icarus and his father, Daedalus, were trying to think of ways to escape from the labyrinth, a palace with intricate corridors, in which they were imprisoned, and they came up with an idea after watching some birds fly past. They collected all the bird feathers they could find and, using wax from candles, they fashioned a pair of wings for Icarus. When Icarus flew out of the labyrinth and away to freedom it looked as if the plan was going well, but Icarus flew too close to the sun, causing the wax to melt and the feathers to fall off, and he came crashing down into the sea below, where an island formed to mark the spot. Icarus, with wings like a bird, represents the soul, and the labyrinth in which he was imprisoned denotes the physical body; once free of the physical body, the soul is able to fly to higher realms. The sun represents the Light or creative forces of the soul, and the air represents the mind. The soul knows what is best for us in any given moment, and by aligning our minds with the creative forces of the soul, we can allow a higher order to guide us through life. If we allow our egos to set our sights and ideals too high, we can get our "wings burned" and be brought back to earth with a bump.

Birds that have feathers but cannot fly, like ostriches and penguins, are also significant. They symbolize the fact that we are souls living on the physical plane, and also that we have to be grounded to Mother Earth so that any spiritual guidance can then, in turn, be grounded into our conscious minds. Just as a lightning conductor absorbs the electricity of a lightning bolt and directs it safely down into the earth, we have to be earthed so that intuitive flashes can be drawn into our being and directed into our consciousness. If we were not grounded, these flashes of creative inspiration would scatter in all directions and not consolidate in us in a meaningful way. This is why it is a good idea for anyone who works in the healing arts and brings guidance through, or for those who wish to receive guidance from their spirit guides or angels, to "ground" themselves first so that any guidance that filters through can then be grounded into the conscious mind, where it can be interpreted and understood. How one goes about grounding before meditating is a matter of choice, but it can be done by imagining a shaft of light coming through the top of the head, down through the center of the body and deep into the ground, almost like a human kebab!

Another way is to picture a large single root coming out of the coccyx area at the base of the spine, and going deep down in to the earth where it spreads out underground like the roots of a large tree; or it can be a long piece of thick rope or chain that anchors you from your coccyx area to the center of the earth. There is no right or wrong way to ground; it is just what appeals to you.

We all know how it feels when we've put on a few pounds in weight – we feel heavy and dumpy – but as soon as the extra weight is shed, we feel lighter and have more of a spring in our step. It is the same when we add an extra few pounds of burdens and worries onto ourselves – we feel energetically weighed down. But as soon as we release these unnecessary burdens, we feel as light as a feather, because we are allowing the *light*ness of our soul, and the *light* of our soul, to flow freely through us. Just as the Egyptian goddess, Ma'at, judged the weight of souls against a feather, if our souls are full of burdens and worries, they become heavy and pull us down. But if our souls are free of physical burdens and worries, they are as light as a feather and can rise up to greater things.

Chapter Eight
Eggs

"Know ye not that ye are the temple of God and that the Spirit of God dwelleth in you?"

I Corinthians 3:16

Birds are said to have evolved from reptiles, and indeed the legs of birds still show reptilian-like scales. Many reptiles lay eggs, and some of the ones that do, desert the eggs once laid, for them to hatch on their own. Birds are different in that they all lay eggs, and being warm-blooded, they sit on their eggs to keep them at a constant temperature until the incubation period is over and the young chicks are hatched. In many bird species, the female and the male take it in turns to sit on the eggs, but in the case of the Emperor penguin, it is the male who patiently stands for two months with the single egg balanced on his feet to keep it from touching the ice and snow, and insulates it with hanging folds of skin.

A bird's egg is made up of three main parts: the outer shell, and the white albumen and yellow yolk inside. A little germinal spot on the yolk grows into the embryo after fertilization, and the developing chick obtains calcium for its growing bones from the shell, its water from the albumen, and its nutrients from the yolk. The shell is also porous to gases so that essential oxygen can permeate into the shell and carbon dioxide can filter out. There is also a small air space at one end of the egg; just before hatching, the young chick will pierce it with its beak in order to get used to breathing air before entering the outside world.

Eggs come in different shapes and sizes. All eggs are basically oval, but some are more rounded while others are more pointed. The eggs of the guillemot, for example, are quite pointed at one end, so that when bumped, the egg will spin around in small circles to minimize the risk of the egg falling off the cliff edge. It is not known why eggs come in

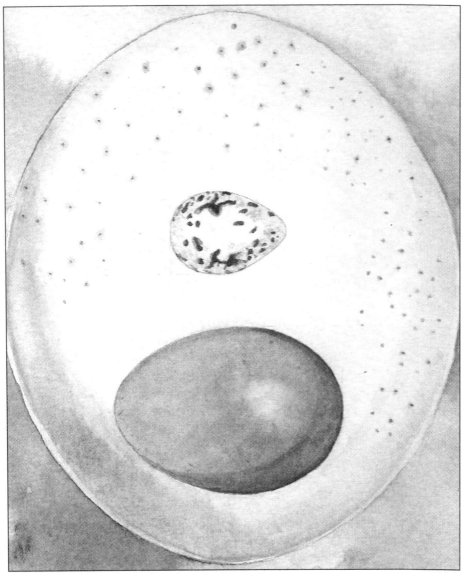

Guillemot's egg (speckled)and hen's egg drawn to scale over an ostrich egg

such a variety of colors and patterns, except as a way to help birds identify their own eggs from others. Eggs of ground-nesting birds are usually of colors similar to the background for camouflage, but other eggs are mysteriously very bright and colorful and are glaringly obvious. Eggs of some babblers (tropical forest birds) are so shiny you can almost see your reflection in them. The smallest eggs laid are those of the smaller hummingbirds, each weighing around 0.02oz, whereas an ostrich egg weighs around 3.3lbs. The ten-foot tall elephant-bird of Malagasy (Madagascar) that was thought to have become extinct in the 17th century, laid eggs weighing around 20 pounds, each containing approximately two gallons of liquid![1]

Humanity has capitalized on the versatility of eggs for centuries. The egg yolk and white have been used extensively as a basic ingredient in cooking, providing a good source of protein, while the inedible shell has been used creatively in artwork where whole shells are decoratively painted, or they are broken into pieces and used in mosaics. Eggs have also been used as a tool for divining the future, a technique known as oomancia, where an egg is broken into a bowl of water and the future told by interpreting the different shapes the white albumen forms. In days gone by, collecting the eggs of wild birds was either a fun pastime, especially among small boys, or a serious business for monetary gain, but nowadays there are strict regulations in most countries about which eggs may be collected and sold, to ensure the continuation of certain species.

Eating eggs used to be seasonal until the domestication of fowls. The modern chicken is a descendant of the Indian jungle fowls that were brought into Europe, the Middle East and China in the second millennium BC by traders, and into the New World by Christopher Columbus in the late 1400's. These fowls were easily domesticated and had the added advantage of being able to produce eggs all year long. Hens' eggs are by far the most popular when it comes to eggs for eating, but other eggs that are eaten around the world include duck, quail, goose, gull, pheasant and ostrich eggs. The largest egg in the modern world is the ostrich egg, equivalent to about twenty hen's eggs, requiring forty minutes to hard boil – wonderful for feeding a lot of people in one sitting, so long as they are not wanting to eat immediately.

The Symbology of Eggs

The Physical Shell

The essential part of an egg, the yolk and albumen, is housed and protected by the shell, and the essential part of us, the soul, can be thought of as being housed and protected by the shell of the physical body. The soul is our divine aspect and our physical body is the temple that houses the Divine.

We incarnate onto the earth plane for our souls to have the opportunity to evolve and grow through the many experiences life on earth has to offer. But our souls have to inhabit a physical body in order to live on the dense physical plane and, as a result, the physical body becomes the vehicle through which the soul operates and expresses itself.

As well as deciding what lessons we would like to learn, the fears we want to master, the gifts and talents we want to use, and the opportunities and experiences we require in this life, we also decide who our parents will be, the ancestral line we are going to be born in to, our genetic traits, the geographical location of our birth, and the exact time of birth – to name but a few things that will be the most conducive to helping us with our life lessons.

Once we have chosen our biological parents, we then need to be "conceived" and a physical body needs to be created for use by our souls in the coming life. From the moment the sperm meets the egg, our souls energetically link with the fertilized egg; as the gestation period begins, an energetic framework of what our physical bodies will look like is first laid down in the womb, around which our physical bodies are modeled. According to Lazaris, the soul takes up residence in the physical body any time during the pregnancy; some souls like to enter right at the beginning of gestation, whereas other souls slip in during or just after birth. Most souls, however, usually enter around the seven-month period of gestation.[2]

Before a soul takes up residence in a physical body it first has to go through a process whereby it gradually loses conscious recollection of the spirit world. This happens because, first of all, the separation from our true home in the spirit world would be too emotionally painful for us. Also, we are given the opportunity to start each new life with fresh eyes so that we are not prejudiced by previous knowledge and inhibitions. If we were to remember everything about the spirit world, including all our past lives, plus this life's challenges, not only would we not be able to cope mentally with all the data, but how would we be able to learn anything if we already knew the answers? But the higher consciousness of our souls, called the Higher Self, still knows every tiny detail, and we can call on our Higher Selves for advice and guidance at any time.

The Auric Shell

Just as the physical body acts as a shell to protect the soul, there is also a "shell" that protects the physical body – an egg-shaped electromagnetic field called an aura.

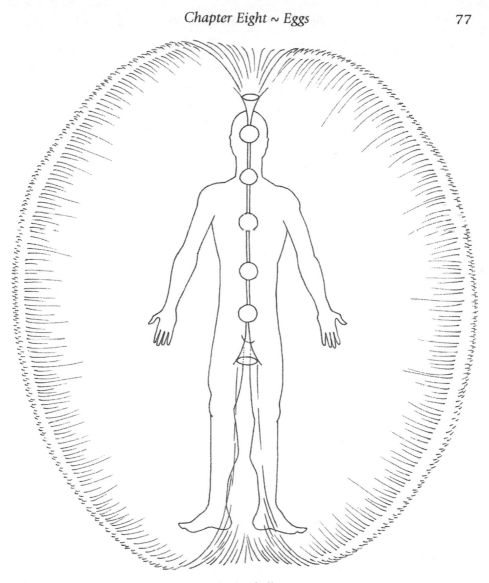

Auric Shell

This electromagnetic field of pulsating energy surrounds the physical body like a shell, extending outwards to protects us. The aura is like a radar, energetically scanning our surroundings and relaying back to us information about our environment. We instinctively know what the atmosphere of a place feels like as soon as we arrive, or whether somebody we meet is feeling sad or happy before they even open their mouths. This is the information picked up by our auras, and as much as people and the environment are broadcasting to us, we are continually broadcasting to them, creating one big auric communication network.

The aura is made up of seven known layers, with each layer having a specific function, and each one vibrating at a faster rate than the one below it, but all interpenetrating and intermingling. The auric layer closest to the physical body is called the etheric body and is associated with our physical sensations; the next is called the emotional body and, as the name suggests, is associated with our human emotions; the third layer is called the mental body and is associated with our individual thoughts; and the last four layers, collectively called the causal body, are associated with the soul and the higher qualities of the soul, where our thoughts and emotions take on a more universal and divine nature.

There are also seven funnel-shaped spinning vortices, known as the major chakras, that are positioned in the head and along the spine, that extend from the etheric body right through all the layers, and are the means by which energy moves from one auric layer to the next. Each major chakra is an energy center that registers certain psychological data pertaining to our spiritual and personal growth. The chakras also take the energies that come through the auric field and break them down into smaller energetic units that feed the physical body and keep it functioning in a healthy state. So the aura, in addition to protecting the physical body, allows the transference of energies to and from the physical body, just as the shell of a bird's egg protects the embryonic chick and allows the transference of oxygen and carbon dioxide in and out of the egg.

Illness, stress, longtime exposure to harmful radiation (cellular phones, microwaves, television or electricity pylons, etc.), long term use of drugs and alcohol, and traumatic shock, can all weaken the auric shell and make the physical body more vulnerable to illnesses. Keeping the aura strong and balanced is therefore important to one's physical well-being.

Because I am very sensitive to the energies around me, I do two very simple exercises every morning, to help keep my aura strengthened. The first is called 'The Hook Up', described in Donna Eden's book, *Energy Medicine:* you place the middle finger of one hand on your forehead between the eyes, and the middle finger of your other hand in your navel. Then with a slight upward pull on the skin at both points, take a deep breath, relax, and hold this position for a minute or two.[3] The second exercise, from Betty Shine's book, *Mind to Mind,* is called the 'Auric Egg': picture a large egg in front of you with a door; walk into the egg, close the door behind you, and sit on the floor, which is covered with cushions; then picture the egg becoming a comfortable impenetrable shell around you, and know in your mind that you are protected for the whole day.[4]

If I feel my aura is a little weakened, then all I do is simply sit in the sun for ten to fifteen minutes, which helps to energize the aura; if I accumulate any negativity in my aura then, in my meditation at night, I visualize myself standing naked under a waterfall, and I feel the water wash away all the negative energy.

Don't be fooled at how easy these exercises are – energy exercises are simple, yet very powerful.

The Silver Cord

The yolk of a bird's egg is attached to the inside of the shell by two cords to help keep the yolk in place; similarly the soul is anchored and connected to the physical body by an invisible cord, often referred to as the silver cord. Every night when we are asleep, our souls leave the physical body, and travel back to the spirit world, where we meet with our guides and angels, our departed loved ones, and souls who have not incarnated. When we have a dream about someone who has already died, we are usually recalling the time we spent with him or her in the spirit world that night. A friend of mine, who had recently lost her job and was in a state about her finances, had a vivid dream one night. She dreamed the telephone rang, and when she got up to answer it, her deceased mother's voice was on the other end, as clear as daylight, telling her to stop worrying because everything was going to be all right. She woke the following morning feeling comforted, and she knew she had really spoken with her mother the previous night.

We also do some form of work during our nightly visits to the spirit world; this can include healing, teaching, looking after the spirit babies, or welcoming back souls who have recently departed the earth. The times when we have had a good night's sleep but wake in the morning feeling just as tired as we did when we went to bed, are usually the nights we have been working hard in the spirit world. When this happens to me, I say to my guides the next night before I go to sleep, 'I don't know what work you've got in store for me tonight, but please make sure I come back into my physical body rested', and that usually does the trick.

Before we wake up, our souls are guided back to our physical body by the silver cord, rather like the guiding rope that directs a deep-sea diver back to the boat. But when a soul has finished its time on earth and physical death has occurred, the silver cord breaks, releasing the soul from the physical body once and for all, to continue its journey back to the spirit world and home. And just as we would throw away an eggshell after removing the essential contents inside, so the soul leaves the empty physical shell behind, as it serves no purpose anymore.

The Cosmic Egg

The egg is an ancient symbol of fertility and the creation of life. All of life is created from a single sphere, regardless of whether this sphere will become a human body or a whole Universe. To get an idea of how a sphere from which life can be created would look, break open a chicken's egg and notice how the yellow yolk, the female aspect of the egg, is a perfectly round circle. A common artifact in many cultures is the egg and the serpent, where the egg represents the female aspect, the serpent represents the male aspect, and together they create new life. In Egyptian hieroglyphics, the symbol of the egg means potentiality, the potential of something coming into being.

Some mythologies speak of the world being derived from a cosmic egg, or of gods being hatched from eggs. In most of these stories, when the cosmic egg split in two, the upper part of the shell became the sky while the lower half became the earth. In Hindu mythology, for example, it was said that the universe was in darkness in the beginning, but the Lord created the waters into which he dropped a seed that grew into a golden egg. After one celestial year, Brahma, the ancestor of all worlds, was hatched from the egg, and the top half of the shell formed the heavens and the bottom half formed the material world.

In Greek mythology, there is the story of a married woman called Leda who was bathing in a stream one day when Zeus approached her in the guise of a swan, and ravished her. That night she slept with her husband, and later she produced two eggs, one hatching Pollux and Helen, fathered by Zeus, and the other egg hatching Castor and Clymenstra, fathered by her husband. Castor and Pollux became well-known twins, one fathered by a god, the other fathered by a mortal, which reflects the fact that we are Divine beings in a physical body. There are many twins mentioned in mythology: Romulus and Remus (Roman), Artemis and Apollo (Greek), Danaus and Aegyptus (Egyptian), Quetzalcoatl and Xolotl (Aztec), Utu and Inanna (Sumerian), and the Biblical Cain and Abel. Twins are symbolic of the dual nature of humanity -- the male/female or yin/yang principle, as well as the spiritual/physical duality.

Easter Eggs

The egg is probably one of the oldest universal symbols of the continuation of life, given the fact that it is shaped like a circle. Everything in life moves in continuous cycles, with no beginning and no end: the planets in our solar system move in a never-ending cycle around the sun; the seasons move in a cycle; day becomes night and night becomes day; and there is birth, life, death and rebirth again – the examples are endless. To be a little more exact, the energies of life move in a spiral, like a coiled spring, or the double helix of the DNA in the cells in our bodies, and as each cycle is completed, one moves either up or down the spiral. But rest assured that humanity is moving up!

Easter is the Christian festival that recognizes the crucifixion of Jesus and the subsequent celebration of his resurrection and ascension into Heaven. It is symbolic of the archetypal pattern of death and rebirth. The precise date of this historical event is not known, but the Roman Emperor Constantine decided in 325 AD that the date for celebrating Easter would be the Sunday immediately after the first full moon of Spring, the season synonymous with rebirth and renewal. The word 'easter' is thought to come from the German pagan goddess of fertility, Ostara, who later became known to the Anglo-Saxons in England as Eostre. In the Western world eggs are very much a traditional part of the celebrations at Easter, with hand-painted hard-boiled eggs as well as commercialized confectionery eggs. The idea of eggs at Easter time derives from early pagan rituals where eggs were given as a symbol of eternal life, and from Egyptian times when eggs were painted in bright spring colors as a symbol of growth and regeneration. So, the next time you give someone a chocolate egg at Easter, don't give it with the thought that it is expected of you – give it with love, as a symbol of eternal life.

Miscellaneous Eggs

Eggs are also used symbolically in the world of sport, usually to denote no score, or zero, in many games. In the game of cricket, for example, a batsman who is out without scoring any runs is said to be out for a duck, and if he is out the very first ball he faces, he is said to be out for a golden duck. The original term was to be out for a "duck's egg", because the zero placed besides his name on the score sheet resembled an egg. In American sports the term "goose egg" is used rather than "duck's egg". In tennis the word "love" is used when a player hasn't scored any points during a game, and is derived from the French word "l'oeuf" meaning "the egg".

In nursery rhymes and fairy tales, there is Humpty Dumpty who was an egg, and then there are all the golden eggs that were laid. In the story of Jack and the Beanstalk, Jack and his mother were so poor that they decided to sell their cow for money. But instead of taking the cow to the market to be sold, Jack met a man along the way and swapped the cow for some magic beans. When he got home, his mother was so furious that she threw the beans out of the window in a rage. The next morning, to their surprise, a huge beanstalk had grown during the night, so tall it reached high into the clouds, and Jack decided to climb it to see where it ended. At the top was a house that belonged to a malevolent giant, who owned a magic hen that laid golden eggs. When the giant was asleep, Jack stole the hen, but before he could escape, the giant woke up and gave chase; Jack managed to get back to the bottom of the beanstalk and chop it down before the giant could catch him. With a hen that laid golden eggs in their possession, Jack and his mother were never poor again. The message in this story is, always take the opportunities that are presented to you, no matter how small or bizarre they seem, and take them without analysis. This is guidance which, if followed with trust, will bring enriching returns.

In Aesop's fable, "The Goose that Laid the Golden Egg", a simple farmer owned a goose that provided him with eggs every day. But one morning when he went to collect the eggs, he found one that was an odd yellow color and very heavy to hold. The farmer was angry and was about to throw the egg away when he took a closer look and saw, to his delight, that the egg was actually made of pure gold. Every morning, without fail, the goose laid a golden egg and, over time, the farmer became very rich by selling the gold. And, the richer he became, the greedier he became, and in his wanting for more and more, the farmer killed the goose to get at all the gold contained inside her. But when he opened up the dead goose, there was nothing inside. Greed is a fear based on insecurity, usually financial insecurity, where there is a lack of trust that the Universe will always provide, no matter what. Everyone has the right to have abundance in their lives. Giving and receiving freely, and being thankful and grateful for what one already has in one's life, are sure ways of attracting more abundance.

It is amazing how one simple egg can symbolically embrace many different aspects of life. Birds as a whole are symbolic of the spiritual qualities and abilities the soul possesses, but the egg is reflective of the more practical connotations the soul has in its relationship with the physical body, and as such provides us with a wonderful analogy.

Chapter Nine
Birds Reflect Our Character

"We must not only give what we have; we must also give what we are."

Desiré-Joseph Mercier (1851–1926),
Belgian prelate and philosopher

Bird Surnames

Before we incarnated, our souls not only decided on who our parents would be and the family surname, but also what first names we were to be given. Parents may think that they are the ones choosing the names for a child, but in fact it is the incoming soul that spiritually guides them as to the names.

Any numerologist will tell you that every letter, and the words that they form, has an energy vibration, and our names are no exception. Our whole name vibrates at a certain energetic resonance, a personal and individualized vibration, which is aligned to our life lessons. When a woman changes her surname after marriage, she changes the vibration of her name to harmonize with the new life lessons that now involve her husband; married women who prefer to keep their maiden names, do so because they still need the vibration of their birth name in their lives. Anybody who has a yearning to change any of their names, instinctively knows that they need a different name or vibration to the one they presently have. A friend of mine, christened Karen, decided when she was in her twenties to spell her name Karin. She felt it was classier and gave her a new image, but simply changing the "e" for an "i" changed the whole vibration of her name. The vibrations of "Karen" served her well while she was growing up, but then, on a deeper level, she knew she had to change the vibration to one that would align her to her future life lessons.

Modern day surnames are derived from various sources, such as the trade an ancestor plied, the type of town or place from which an ancestor originated, or a person to whom they were related. One can only surmise that a surname of a bird originated from an ancestor keeping such a bird as a pet, or the ancestor being nicknamed after a bird whose attributes he displayed, or the ancestor belonging to a clan that had that particular bird as its symbol or totem.

One day many years ago, when I was working in the outpatient department of a hospital in England, the receptionist called me over and showed me the list of patients that were currently being treated. Nearly half of them had surnames of birds: Mrs Wren, Mrs Robin, Mr Swan, Mr Pidgeon (sic), Mr Parrott (sic), Mr Starling, Mrs Swift, Mrs Martin, Mr Finch, and so on. It seemed that everybody who had a surname of a bird needed treatment at the same time, and although the whole department had a good laugh about it, remarking that it was like working in an aviary, it was nevertheless quite uncanny.

People who have a surname of a bird, whether by birth or by marriage, will often show certain symbolic characteristics of that bird, or of the message it brings. A good example is Florence *Nightingale*, a famous nurse in the Crimean War. During the war, she was kept busy all day marshalling her nurses, tending to the sick and wounded soldiers, doing battle herself with the doctors and the British government in an effort for them to adopt her recommendations to create a more sanitary hospital environment, and trying to get supplies and provisions amid bureaucratic red tape. At night she kept statistics and wrote numerous letters, mainly to the British government to report on the debacle of the standards of the British hospitals in the Crimean area, and she also found time to go around the makeshift wards by lamplight, sitting with any soldier who was awake and comforting him. The majority of Florence Nightingale's pioneering work was done after the Crimean War, where she completely revamped military and civilian hospitals, and started an international nursing college to ensure all nurses were properly and skillfully trained.

The nightingale bird is known for its rich, melodious song, singing all night and sometimes during the day, too, and it is associated with bards and poets who can express themselves beautifully through words and song. Florence Nightingale was active and vociferous both night and day, and after the war her work was conducted chiefly through her writings, in which she had a talent for expressing herself beautifully. The message of a nightingale is HOPE. Florence Nightingale was a great visionary who never gave up hope in her dream of reforming hospitals, no matter how many obstacles she encountered throughout her life. She also instilled hope into the hearts of many people by her continuous fighting for the welfare of the sick and their right to an established health system.

The nightingale bird is a member of the thrush family, the Mother archetype, and Florence Nightingale became a "mother away from home", not only to the soldiers but to many of the nurses and doctors, as well. In Christianity, the nightingale's song was considered to be a yearning for heaven, and Florence Nightingale spent her whole life striving to attain perfect conditions for army and civilian hospitals alike. Florence Nightingale's father was actually born William Shore, but he changed his name to that of an uncle, Peter Nightingale, who had left him a fortune in his will. Was this name change inspired from higher realms so that his daughter would emulate the bird with which she shared a surname, and because she needed that name's vibration to enable her to do the work she came here to do?

Another example of how a bird surname symbolically fits the person is Calamity Jane, the well-known American frontierswoman, immortalized in the 1953 film of the same name starring Doris Day. Calamity Jane's real name was Martha Jane *Canary*. Born in Missouri and brought up in different mining camps across the United States, her parents died when she was quite young. Left on her own, she wandered from place to place, taking any job she could find to try to support herself. She loved to dress in men's clothes, and she became an accomplished horse rider and a master at handling rifles and revolvers. Because of her extensive knowledge of the frontier, she became a scout for the United States army, but many of the stories of her wild and daring adventures were of her own fabrication. In her early twenties, she moved to Deadwood in the Black Hills of South Dakota during the gold rush, and when smallpox broke out a few years later, she was praised for the invaluable help she gave smallpox victims. She toured with Wild West shows before eventually succumbing to alcoholism and an early death.

Canaries sing a much more prettier song in captivity than in the wild, and they are always replacing their song with a new one. Calamity Jane only "sang her songs" – bragging about her adventures – when she was surrounded by people, and she was always replacing her "songs" with more exaggerated and grander tales.

The message of a canary is COMPANIONSHIP. Calamity Jane seemed to be a person who had no sense of where she truly belonged in life, and had a desperate need to fit in somewhere. Esoterically speaking, people who are like this generally have a problem with their root chakra, (the energy vortex at the base of the spine), where they literally cannot seem to put roots down into mother earth to create a sense of stability and security. As a result, they can drift from place to place, or from person to person, trying to find where they belong, and to find the support they don't feel they can give themselves. Calamity Jane's childhood was spent moving from town to town for her father to find work, and later she roamed the frontier. She dressed to shock people into noticing her, and the elaborate stories she told about her heroic deeds and great adventures were an attempt to fit in. She was always seeking companionship, someone to whom she could tell her tales, and people who would act as a surrogate family and a support group for her.

Another bird surname is that of Christopher *Wren*, who was a gifted English architect, mathematician and astronomer, who became known for his architectural designs of several London churches, most notably St. Paul's cathedral. The son of a rector, Wren showed a keen interest in mathematics and astronomy from an early age, and started his career as a professor of astronomy. He later turned his attention to architecture because he felt the current designs of buildings lacked the combination of beautiful art with the precision of science. After a period in France where he studied French architectural designs, particularly of domed churches, he returned to England, where shortly afterwards the Great Fire of London in 1666 reduced two-thirds of the city to ashes. In his capacity as the King's Surveyor of Works, Wren was commissioned to re-design fifty-one of the eighty-seven churches destroyed by the fire, including St. Paul's cathedral, which took thirty-five years to rebuild.

The wren is a small energetic bird that is quite inconspicuous except for his loud song. The message of a wren is SELF-WORTH. Self-worth is recognizing, acknowledging and owning our talents and capabilities. When we have a true sense of self-worth, we do not go around looking for praise and approval from others. We are able to work quietly behind the scenes, deriving personal pleasure and satisfaction from knowing that we are producing work to the best of our abilities.

Christopher Wren had many talents and not only was aware of them, but put them all into practice at some time in his life. He gave his best to everything he did, but his modesty didn't allow him to seek the limelight or to look for recognition for his work. His motive was to produce admirable architectural designs that were visually aesthetic and could be enjoyed for generations to come; whether people attached his name to these buildings was not important to him. Although Wren worked quietly and efficiently behind the scenes, he wasn't shy in voicing his needs. While St. Paul's cathedral was being built, some members of the British government complained that it was taking far too long, because it was already twenty-two years since work had begun and it still wasn't near completion. So, as an incentive, they decided to suspend half of Wren's salary in a bid to speed things up. It took another thirteen years before the cathedral was completed, by which time Wren had to petition for the rest of the monies that were rightly owed to him.

Christopher Columbus, the great mariner and explorer, discovered the New World in 1492 under the aegis of Spain. Born in Italy of Spanish-Jewish descent, he started sailing the seas at an early age and became fascinated with the concept of sailing west as a new way to reach Asia. He eventually put his ideas to the King and Queen of Spain, and doggedly pursued them for a number of years to accept his proposals. Not getting anywhere, he then turned his proposals to demands – he wanted to be knighted, he wanted to be made grand admiral and viceroy, and he wanted ten percent of all takings within his admiralty. The royal court was shocked at first at his audacity but finally conceded, and agreed to finance the voyage. Over the next twelve years, Columbus made four voyages to the west; even though he never reached Asia, he did discover the various West Indian and Central American islands, where he established settlements. Unfortunately, where he excelled as a mariner, he failed as governor of these new Spanish colonies, making enemies locally and in Spain through his egotistical and autocratic behavior. He was even brought back to Spain in chains after his third voyage.

"Columbus" is Latin for *pigeon;* the message of the pigeon is OBEDIENCE and its archetype the Rebel. Christopher Columbus was a man who knew his own mind, and hated to be supervised. He did not like to be told what to do and seldom listened to the advice of others. Yet he always felt his life was divinely guided and saw "signs" in everything that happened to him. When his ships set out on the first voyage, his crew became restless and threatened to become mutinous as weeks passed and no land was seen, and when the captain of the second ship suggested to Columbus that they should change course and sail southwesterly, he refused. Columbus changed his mind when he saw flocks of birds flying towards the southwest, and ordered everybody to sail in that direction as if it had been his own idea in the first place. Very soon land was spotted and the New World was discovered. Columbus thought nothing of disobeying royal orders given to him, but when any member of his crew, the settlers or the natives disobeyed *his* orders, he meted out cruel punishment, including public executions, which eventually led to his downfall as governor of the Indies. The King and Queen of Spain realized Columbus was a poor governor but recognized him as a great mariner and pioneer who discovered lands far beyond their imagination. And, like his namesake, the pigeon, no matter how far he traveled, he always managed to successfully find his way home.

Some Other Bird Names

St. Teresa of Avila was often referred to as the *"Eagle* and *Dove"*, which epitomized her character. A popular saint, she was famous for her visions and mystical experiences, and for becoming the first female Doctor of the Church. Born to aristocratic parents, she was educated at the Augustinian convent in Avila but had to quit after a few years due to ill health. During her convalescence at home, she read the letters of St. Jerome that inspired a religious fervor in her and encouraged her to enter convent life. She eventually joined the Carmelite order in Avila but had to temporarily retire due to ill health again. When she re-entered, she soon became disillusioned with the convent because of the free and easy lifestyle of the nuns; not wanting to fall into the same trap, she started training herself in the discipline of mental prayers. This led to mystical experiences and visions which, although frightening at first, gave her the impetus to focus more on Christ's passion and on what it meant to be a devoted nun. She started to implement a reform in the Carmelite order, reverting to its original principles of devotion and discipline, and opened the St. Joseph's convent in Avila after approval from the Pope. It was known as the community of the Discalced (without shoes, or barefoot) Carmelites. Here, leading by example, she enforced strict rules and a disciplined spiritual life, encouraging only those to enter the order who were willing to work hard towards humility and holiness. She went on to establish many new convents and, with the help of St. John of the Cross, started the male side of the Carmelite order. She traveled extensively throughout Spain and left a legacy of writings, including *The Way of Perfection* and her autobiography.

As mentioned before, the message of an eagle is POWER and STRENGTH, and a dove's is PEACE. Teresa of Avila lacked physical strength in her early years, but she more than made up for it with spiritual strength in her later years. Initially she strove to be admired by other people, but soon she realized that this was holding her back. She then had a profound vision of the wounded Christ, which motivated her to move all thoughts away from selfish aggrandizement. The kind of discipline of mental prayer she developed required an enormous amount of strength, resolution, and tenacity; the effort paid off with the self-empowerment she eventually attained. And with the internal power came inner peace and contentment. Her many visions and mystical experiences, and the setting up of new convents to advocate her ideals and principles, met with a lot of opposition and criticism. But her inner strength and belief in her ideals fuelled an external power that kept her moving toward her dreams through all the adversity, balanced by her affectionate and peaceable nature.

The message of a *robin* is PROTECTION, and the legendary outlaw of Sherwood Forest, Robin Hood, made it his mission in life to protect the poor people of the land. In AA Milne's books on Winnie the Pooh, Christopher Robin was the guardian and protector of his many animal friends.

Birds as Pets

In theory, any bird can be tamed and kept in captivity, but only a handful have been successfully domesticated. Chickens, turkeys, geese, ducks and ostriches are usually kept to provide meat, eggs and feathers; pigeons, falcons and hawks are usually kept for recreational sports; and finches, canaries and birds in the parrot family are usually kept as pets.

The type of bird we choose to have around us, as in a pet, is significant, because the message attached to that bird is very often reflected in our personality. These traits may be obvious, or they may be dormant and need to be expressed; sometimes the shadow side of the trait is more dominant in the personality, or the positive aspect appears in certain areas of our lives and not in others.

The message of a peacock is HONESTY, and people who keep peacocks tend to be straightforward, honest and sincere people, or they have the inherent ability to be so; sometimes, however, the shadow side may be more apparent and these people can come over as too frank and tactless with their opinions, which can be hurtful to others. The message of a finch is COMPROMISE, and people who keep finches are usually able to achieve the balance of give and take in life, and are able to meet others halfway for the benefit of all. If the shadow side is more evident, they either give too much or take too much in life. The message of a pigeon is OBEDIENCE with the archetype of the Rebel. People who keep pigeons are usually very dutiful, amenable, and respectful of others, and they like to do everything by the book. If the shadow side of their nature is more noticeable, they come across as always wanting to do things their way without listening to the advice of others.

The message of a chicken is PATIENCE, and people who keep chickens tend to be patient, uncomplaining people who allow things to happen when they are supposed to happen, or at the very least have an inherent ability to be patient even if they are not yet using this quality in their lives. In Africa, the chicken is very popular in many native communities. Nearly every village keeps chickens, not only as a favorite food, but also for use in rituals and as sacrificial offerings. Many black Africans seem to have the patience of a saint; I have seen how they can stand in queues for hours on end, sometimes all day, without a word of complaint.

One person I know loves to show off his expensive material acquisitions as a way of trying to prove he is better than others. He keeps rare live ducks in an aviary in his garden, bragging to anybody who visits how much each duck cost to purchase. His choice of keeping ducks with their message of FAITH, as opposed to any other bird, is reflecting his inner need to have more faith in himself. If he believed in himself and became aware of his true qualities and inner strengths, he would lose the need to impress other people with material things.

By far the most popular birds bred as caged pets or for an aviary are those of the parrot family. These include parrots, macaws, cockatiels, cockatoos, parakeets and budgerigars. Members of the parrot family come in different sizes and colors, but all share the common feature of short, hooked bills, with the upper bill attached to the skull by a flexible joint that permits free up and down movement of the upper beak. This is very symbolic as the message of a parrot is COMMUNICATION. Keeping one of the parrot family as a pet often reflects the owner's ability to be a good communicator, either in speech or in writing; it can also indicate a person who is very talkative, or it can represent the opposite where someone prefers to let others do all the talking – or they are gossips! Long John Silver's parrot, Captain Flint, in Robert Louis Stevenson's book, *Treasure Island*, certainly did a lot of the talking for him, and Sir Winston Churchill, who had obvious communicating skills as a politician and statesman, had a pet African gray parrot and a budgerigar called Toby; he often wore feathers from the latter in his cap. Churchill also kept ducks and black swans at his home in Chartwell in Kent, England, and he certainly instilled faith (duck) in the people of Britain to bring the nation out of the darkest years of World War II, a war (like all wars) that brought transformation (swan) to Britain and the rest of the world.

Sometimes even birds that we did not specifically buy as a pet become a part of our lives for a long term, and the message of the bird is still reflected in our personalities.

A friend of mine found an injured mousebird in her garden, and after she nursed it back to health it became a tame pet. The message of a mousebird is PRUDENCE, and this friend exercises common sense and care in most areas of her life except where her finances are concerned. Throwing caution to the wind, she spends money she doesn't have and is often in debt. The mousebird coming into her life on a long-term basis was reflecting her prudent/rash behavioral patterns, and perhaps it is suggesting that she can extend her inherent prudent nature into the financial side of her life, as well.

The most famous prisoner on Alcatraz Island in San Francisco Bay was Robert Stroud, better known as the "Birdman of Alcatraz". While in a prison in Kansas where he was serving life imprisonment for murder, he found an injured canary in the recreation ground. As a result of taking care of this bird, his interest in canaries grew to the point where, after being granted permission by the prison authorities to breed and study them in a makeshift laboratory in an adjoining cell, he became an expert in canary behavior and diseases. When he was moved to the prison on Alcatraz to serve out the rest of his life sentence, he was already known as the "Bird Doctor" and was allowed to continue his breeding and study programmes with canaries. Of the fifty-two years he stayed in prison, most of them were in solitary confinement because of his violent behavior, so the canary (COMPANIONSHIP) was an apt bird to have come into his life.

The word "alcatraz" means pelican in Spanish, and the message of a pelican is ADAPTABILITY. Alcatraz prison harbored hardened criminals, many of whom were unable to adapt to the laws of the land (which put them behind bars in the first place) and were misfits in society (the shadow side of adaptability). Once incarcerated, they had to literally adapt to life in prison, where strict rules and regulations were forced upon them.

The length of time a bird stays in our lives is not important, but the type of bird and its message are significant. The bird may be reminding us that we have a particular characteristic or trait that needs to be developed for our benefit as well as for others, or it could be that we need to tone down the shadow side of that trait. Sometimes the bird is informing us of hidden talents we didn't know we had and telling us that now is the time to put them into action.

If you have a surname of a bird, whether by birth or by marriage, or when a bird comes into your life, either by choice or by design, take a moment to see how the symbolic meaning of that particular bird applies to your life or your character.

Chapter Ten
Putting the Messages to Practical Use

"You must hear the bird's song without attempting to render it into nouns and verbs."

Ralph Waldo Emerson (1803–82),
American essayist and poet

Angels have been appearing to humans since time immemorial, conveying messages of wisdom, guidance, warnings and encouragement. Not only are there numerous accounts of angelic encounters in religious texts the world over, but many modern day writers like Diana Cooper and Doreen Virtue are reawakening us to the presence of angels. But it is not commonly known that birds are also part of the angelic realm and as such are spiritual messengers, too. Unlike their heavenly counterparts, though, birds are readily visible and tangible, and they are abundantly seen, and when they seek our attention in order to deliver a spiritual message, it's as if their message has been hand delivered.

The angelic realm and the spirit world understand that we humans have been blessed with the power of free will, and therefore angelic beings will never interfere in the plan of our souls. We are responsible for our lives and what goes on in them, and it is important for us to make our own choices and decisions. But if the heavens feel we are straying from our spiritual paths, or that we are blocking ourselves from moving forward in our lives, a spiritual message will be sent to us one way or another.

Over and above the general symbology surrounding birds as a whole, each bird carries a specific message, a keyword. The bird with the most relevant message we need to hear at any given time will make its presence known to us in some way, and once we know the keyword, it is then up to us to apply that message to our lives, because it has been divinely given to us for our benefit.

Birds convey their messages to us in myriad ways, including through dreams, by acting out of character in our presence, by becoming part of our lives as pets, or through our having an affinity for a particular bird.

Messages of Birds to which we have an Affinity

Some people have an attraction and love for one particular bird. Collecting ornamental owls is a common favorite, and I know at least two people who collect ornaments and artifacts of guinea fowls because of a love for these birds. Others who have an affinity for ravens and crows enjoy collecting stories, poems and pictures of them. In many ways, these birds have become their personal totem.

An attraction for a particular bird is really an underlying attraction to the message, or the archetypal pattern, that bird holds. One lady I know who loves owls and has ornaments of owls all over her house finds that people are often asking her for advice and relying on her wisdom (the message of the owl); another person I know who also has a love of owls and collects them, wishes she could be more wise in her decision-making because she has a tendency to act first and think afterwards.

The message of a guinea fowl is STABILITY, and one of the people I know who collects artifacts of this bird has a rocky marriage and a depressive personality. Surrounding herself with her guinea fowl ornaments reflects her underlying need for stability in her life.

People who have an affinity to crows identify with the shape-shifter archetype. Shamans of many cultural tribes are known to be able to temporarily change their physical appearance (or shape-shift) when they move into a different level of consciousness. It is the same phenomenon, called transfiguration, that occasionally happens when spiritual mediums take on the features, and sometimes the mannerisms, of the spirit guide or deceased relative they are channeling at the time.

On a practical level, shape-shifting is representative of the many faces we have to our personality; in this respect, people who relate to the archetype of the crow tend to have an adaptable personality and they are able to relate easily to all kinds of different people. Conversely, people who show the shadow side of the crow are those who tend not to be consistent in their beliefs, changing their opinions depending on whom they're with at the time.

Companies that use a bird as their logo are also identifying their businesses with the messages of that bird.

When a Bird Acts out of Character

When a bird wants to convey a message to us, it will try to catch our attention by *acting out of character*. If we are sitting at the coast and a flock of gulls flies overhead, there is nothing unusual about this; similarly, when we see birds hopping around the garden feeding on worms and insects, sitting in trees and shrubs singing, or splashing around in the bird bath, this is normal behavior. It is when they behave in unusual ways that we have to take note.

Several months ago I was chatting to a patient as he was about to get into his car that was parked under a large tree. Sunbirds are often in this tree, but on this particular afternoon, one of the male sunbirds suddenly dive-bombed my patient, not once, but three times, causing him to leap out of the way every time. Sunbirds fly in a flittering, darting manner, but dive-bombing people is not one of their characteristics. It was clear this little bird was trying to get my patient's attention by acting out of character. This young man had broken up with his girlfriend several months ago and had since made himself quite reclusive by shunning any kind of social life. He was miserable, but the sunbird, whose message is JOY and HAPPINESS, was telling him it was time he found joy and happiness in his life once more. I explained that the likelihood of joy and happiness coming to knock on his front door was remote, so it was up to him to go out and create it for himself. If it was too painful for him to go back to the places he used to frequent with his former girlfriend, then he should find new places to go where he could make new friends. I told him that life was for living, and joy and happiness were everyone's heritage and divine right, and the sooner he stepped out of the self-pity frame, the sooner he would be happy again.

A friend of mine who is wheelchair bound phoned me one day to say that while she had been sitting in her bedroom that morning she had noticed two birds acting strangely, right outside her window. She said that a little weaver bird kept jumping on and off the back of a dove, in a way that seemed to be trying to attract her attention. She knew they had a message for her but didn't know what it was. This is indeed strange behavior; I've never known two different species of birds to interact in such a manner. The message of a weaver bird is CONSOLIDATION and its archetype is the Weaver, and the dove, as we know, is PEACE. I told her that there was some area of her life where things appeared to be falling apart at the seams. I said she was being told that she needed to consolidate either her efforts or the people around her because, unless there was unity, there would not be any peace. She said she knew exactly what the message was implying, because she had started a successful business providing homes for people in need, including AIDS orphans. But recently the staff who were helping her in this scheme all seemed to want to run the show in their own way, and as a result there was mayhem and a lot of infighting. She realized she was being told that, if she wanted to continue to build up her business and life mission, she had to take over the reins firmly once more and bring the staff back under her guidance and command so that things could run in a constructive and peaceful way.

We mustn't start thinking that every bird that flies past the window or sits on the roof of our house is conveying a message. A one-off sighting of a bird not normally seen in the garden doesn't necessarily mean there is a message, either, because birds can be thrown off course in their migration flights or can literally decide to take a new route that might entail stopping off in our garden for a break along the way. Also, the ecology around us is constantly changing, so new birds move into suburban areas while other familiar garden birds move out. The first bird we hear singing in the morning or the last bird we hear in the evening is not significant, nor is hearing a commotion in the garden as a group of sparrows fight over a piece of bread.

However, if a bird flies into the house, dive-bombs us, persistently hovers around, comes and sits next to us, raps on a window, or displays any other unusual behavior, then we must be alert to the possibility that a message is being brought to us.

Dreams

The unconscious mind speaks to us through our dreams, usually in symbols. In comparatively modern times, through psychoanalysis and dream interpretation, the importance of the unconscious mind has been realized. Working with dreams and understanding their meanings is very important, as they can help us to understand our lives and ourselves better. They help us to discover the inner beliefs, thoughts, emotions, wishes and fears that are buried deep in our unconscious mind, of which we are seldom consciously aware.

Dreams can convey all sorts of messages: they can be inspirational and creative; be prophetic; give us warnings; give us ideas on how to solve a problem; give us guidance, wisdom or advice. Dreams are also very individual – a certain symbol in a dream will mean one thing to one person but will convey a completely different meaning to another. The late Nerys Dee, a well-known dream analyst, described dreams as "highly personal messages from ourselves to ourselves".[1] A dream symbol very often has a general meaning, but how it is applied to one's life depends on the individual and their life circumstances. For example, water in dreams generally represents the emotions, but the exact state and type of emotion involved depends on the rest of the dream, the individual's personality, and what they are going through at the time.

Another way birds bring messages to us is in our dreams, and are a type of dream symbol. Knowing the keyword of the bird depicted in the dream can help us to analyze the dream and decipher the message it contains.

One of my patients, Jeff, dreamed one night that he was meeting his wife for lunch at a very exclusive restaurant, but when she walked in, she was carrying a penguin under her arm! Throughout lunch, this penguin misbehaved and walked all over the table knocking things onto the floor, and Jeff was furious with his wife for embarrassing him, especially as there were some influential business associates of his dining at the same restaurant. The message of a penguin is RESPONSIBILITY. In real life, Jeff was a workaholic, working day and night, and very often neglecting his family. He was taking on too much responsibility at work, more than his fair share, but he didn't want to say no to his bosses for fear of being demoted in the firm or asked to leave. At the same time, he was neglecting his responsibilities on the home front, and his wife and children were feeling almost abandoned. The penguin came into his dream to alert him to revise where his true responsibilities lay, before it was too late and he lost everything.

What to do when we get a Message

When you realize that a bird is conveying a message to you, go to the Appendix at the end of this book and look up the keyword for that bird. Then take a moment to see how that message applies to your life at that particular time. The message will either be relevant to your life in general, or it will be relevant to one particular area of your life. The message comes in the form of advice or guidance, and because it has been divinely given to you to help you with your life, the most important step is then to act on the advice or guidance.

Just as dream symbols have a common meaning but each symbol has a personal, individualized message for every dreamer, which influences how it is applied to that person's life, so it is with the keywords of birds. You have to apply the message to *your* life. The message of a penguin, RESPONSIBILITY, may mean to one person that they need to learn to be more responsible in certain aspects of their life; to another person, that they are taking on too much responsibility, shouldering other people's problems as well as their own. The message of a heron, SOLITUDE, may mean to one person that they have become reclusive and need to socialize more, but to another person it may mean they need to get away from the rat race of life and have some quiet time alone.

A bird's message is always relevant to what is going on in your life at that point in time. It may simply be giving you advice on what to do in a current situation, and in this respect its guidance is often quite obvious. Anne, an acquaintance, was in a constant worry about her financial affairs – so much so, that she was having difficulty sleeping at night and was in a state because she didn't know what to do or which way to turn. One day when she felt she was at the end of her tether, a dove flew into her house. It was literally telling her that she had to find PEACE of mind because, until she did, she wouldn't be able to think logically about her situation or be able to access any intuitive guidance. Similarly, the cuckoo that came to me with his message of TRUST just before I went to America, was telling me simply to trust that there was a higher reason for my going, even if I didn't consciously know why.

Other times, the bird may be advising you on a negative thought pattern that is stopping you from moving forward in life. In this case, it may not be so obvious how the message applies to your life, and it may be necessary to take the keyword and look at every aspect of its meaning before its message becomes clear. If it still isn't clear, it is more than likely because you are not being as honest with yourself as you could be about your shortcomings.

Julie, a former patient, dreamed one night of a woodpecker, the message of which is SECURITY. She couldn't understand what the message implied and was adamant the message wasn't for her because, as far as she was concerned, she felt very secure in life. She was happily married, she and her husband lived comfortably, and they had no debts. If she analyzed her life more deeply, she would have realized that she was a person who tried to control everything around her because, on a deeper level, she didn't feel safe and secure in the world. When she was growing up, her parents didn't give her the emotional support she felt she needed, which led to an underlying belief that she was unable to support herself financially and emotionally as an adult. As a result, she relied on external sources, like cigarettes, money in the bank, and her husband, to give her the emotional and financial security she needed. But these external means were only giving her a false sense of security, because they could not be guaranteed to be permanent. The woodpecker in her dream was advising her that it was time for her to address these underlying fears of insecurity, and to start developing a sense of inner security.

When a bird suddenly makes its presence known, for example by flying into your house or coming to sit next to you, make a note if you can as to what you were thinking or talking about at the precise moment the bird appeared. Sometimes the bird is giving you confirmation, or added food for thought, regarding what you were thinking about. A friend told me that during her coffee break at work one day, she decided to sit outside on the little stone wall on the patio outside her office. As she sat in the warm sunshine, her mind mulled over many things, but when she began to ponder whether she should try for a newly-vacated position at work that meant an internal promotion, and deciding she probably wasn't good enough for the job, a starling suddenly flew down to a puddle that was right next to her foot. The starling drank from the puddle, then looked at her for a while before flying off. The message of a starling is CONFIDENCE, and it appeared at the precise moment when she was deliberating whether she was good enough to apply for the promotion. The starling was telling her to have more confidence in her abilities, and to go for the new job.

Invoking Help from Birds

As we can invoke traditional angels to help us in any given situation, we can call on a specific bird whenever we feel we need the attributes of that bird's message to help us through a particular point in our lives. Say, for example, a situation arises where you need to be more trusting: sit quietly, close your eyes, and take three deep breaths to relax. Picture a cuckoo in your mind and ask the cuckoo to help you to be more trusting in that situation. Know that the help is forthcoming, and then thank the cuckoo for its help. Similarly, if you are needing strength in a given situation, call on an eagle in the same way; if you are needing to forgive someone, call on a hummingbird to help you; if you are needing to be more practical and grounded, call on an ostrich, and so on. If you have difficulty visualizing a particular bird, or the bird whose help you require is not found in your country and you have no idea what it looks like, it doesn't matter, because you can just call on that bird by name and you will receive the desired help – for example, "I call on a bulbul to help me be more ambitious". One doesn't need to go into a great ceremony of lighting candles next to a picture of the bird you are invoking for help – all it takes is a simple and respectful request.

The Finer Points

Obviously, birds that suddenly appear next to you or fly into your house are going to be those birds commonly found in your particular area. If you were in the middle of London, England, for example, you wouldn't expect to see an ostrich ambling up your garden path, or a flamingo sitting on your washing line. (If this does happen, the only message here is that you probably shouldn't have had that extra glass of wine at lunch!). Every bird has a specific message, and the most pertinent message you need to hear at any given time will always be delivered in some way. If the bird with that message is not found in your area, then the bird will perhaps appear in a dream, or maybe even on a card that you have been sent.

The number of birds conveying a message at any given time should be taken into consideration. We saw this in the story of my patient Susan (chapter two) when she dreamed of three owls and was later pestered by three crows in the park. This informed her that she was holding on to three negative belief patterns that now had to be addressed in order to bring significant changes to her life. As a general guideline, I have found that when one, two or three birds of the same species appear at the same time, it usually indicates one, two or three different areas of our lives to which their message or keyword applies. But when more than three birds of the same species appear at any given time, it is usually just a reinforcement of the message, to hammer it home, so to speak. If, for example, you dreamed of two peacocks, it means there are two areas in your life where you need to be more honest with yourself, or there are two people in your life with which you need to be more honest.

One of my neighbours phoned me a while ago to say there were fifteen crows sitting in the tree just outside her front door, and making a tremendous noise as if they were trying to get her attention. They *were* trying to get her attention because this lady was in an extremely unhappy marriage that was beginning to make her physically ill, and as she wasn't listening to her own gut feelings that she had to move out and move on with her life, the crows, with their message of CHANGE, were sent *en masse* to bring the message home to her that it was now imperative she made changes, otherwise the changes would be made for her.

Also, when more than one type of bird brings a message, either together or within a short period of time of each other, string the messages of each bird together, before applying them to your life. This usually happens when the birds want to pass on a more involved message and one keyword isn't sufficient to impart exactly what they want to tell you. A good example of this is in the story above of my friend who saw the weaver bird piggybacking the dove; seen individually, the keyword of each bird wasn't conveying enough information for her to understand what she had to do, but together they helped her understand that she had to unite her work staff so they could work together in a more peaceable way.

Another friend had a dream one night where she was anxiously trying to find in her roof a swift's nest that she knew was there but couldn't locate. The next morning she received an unexpected card in the post from a cousin who lived overseas, enquiring how she was, and on the front of the card was a big picture of ducks. The message of a swift is FREEDOM and the message of a duck is FAITH. This friend felt trapped in a job she hated, and she wanted to get out and start her own business from home using her sewing skills. But she stayed in this state of limbo because she was worried that she wouldn't be able to earn a living from her sewing, even though this was where her heart was. These two birds, coming in tandem, were telling her that she had lost her freedom by insisting on tying herself to a job in which she knew she wasn't happy, and that she was to have more faith in her abilities, and to have faith that everything would turn out well in her new venture because she was following her heart and her intuition, and now was the time to go after what she really wanted to do in life.

Home to Roost

We are all on a spiritual journey. The quest of our souls is to remember our Divine heritage, and to spiritually grow so that we can eventually become one with the Divine again, in mind and in purpose.

In order to grow spiritually, there are lessons we need to learn and fears we need to master, and we have chosen which specific ones we wish to work on in any given lifetime. But when we first come into our physical bodies we are purposely made unaware of what these lessons might be, and the fun part (although some people may call it a challenge) is to discover what we're here to learn.

But how can it be fun when our relationships don't work, we're unhappy in our jobs, or we have an illness? It is in these unpleasant situations that the clues lie. We are co-creators with God, and we are here on the earth plane to create. Looking at our lives, and what we have created so far, gives us an indication of the life lessons and the fears we have chosen to work on. The areas of our lives that are not working as well as we would like, are the areas we are creating according to negative beliefs. These fears and negative beliefs were seeded and took root in our childhoods, and then kept in motion by our habitual ways of thinking. Our job is to unearth these negative beliefs, find out where they stem from, forgive the people involved, forgive ourselves, and let go of the negative belief. Then not only do we start to spiritually grow, we begin to create lives that are happy, joyous, and full of love. When we realize that we are spiritual beings having a human experience, and not human beings having a spiritual experience, will put things into better perspective. And by healing ourselves in this way, we also start to heal the planet.

The energies on this planet are changing and human consciousness is rising. This means that our individual power has now shifted to our conscious minds, and we are being given the opportunity to be masters of our own lives. We are beginning to awaken to the fact that we have been creating our lives all along, unconsciously, but with this new understanding we can now take charge. Whatever we do not like about our lives, we can consciously change; we can consciously root out offending belief patterns and release them, and consciously make more wise choices and decisions that will bring positive results. Gone are the days when we could blame God for "our lot" in life, or blame our parents and anybody else, for our adult lives not working smoothly. Mastering our lives means creating all aspects of our lives responsibly and with conscious thought.

We are surrounded by a natural world of teachers that are not only there to help us to unlock the mysteries of the Universe, but to help us individually to become more consciously aware of what our life lessons are, to help us find the mental blocks that are spiritually holding us back, and to help us discover the gifts we have brought with us to share with others.

Birds are part of this natural world of teachers. They are divine messengers, and they are there to give us inspiration, encouragement and guidance. The messages birds have for us are divinely given, to help us to spiritually grow, and are not meant to criticize or judge us; they are always brought to us with love. We are in charge of our lives, but as we move along our spiritual journeys, there is always plenty of divine guidance around us.

As part of the angelic realm, and therefore part of the Divine, birds are very special. I hope this book has helped you to understand this and given you some guidance for moving forward into a more positive life.

Appendix

There are nearly nine thousand known species of birds alive in the world today so, for obvious reasons, I have had to be selective!

I have chosen a wide global representation of birds that are the most likely to be encountered. These include the more common birds found in Australia, Great Britain, North America and South Africa, as well as universally-known birds such as the puffin, penguin and albatross. The birds are listed in alphabetical order, along with the message each bird brings and the archetype it embraces where applicable, followed by a short description of the message.

The common names by which birds are known around the world can sometimes be misleading. A bird in one country might share the same common name with a bird in another country, but in fact they are two completely different species of bird, and therefore they bring separate messages.

In this regard, the ones to look out for, pertaining to this book, are as follows:

- The warblers found in North America are a different family to the warblers found in Australia, Great Britain, and South Africa. Their messages are listed under AMERICAN WARBLER and WARBLER, respectively.

- The flycatchers found in North America are a different family to the flycatchers found in Australia, Great Britain and South Africa. Their messages are listed under AMERICAN FLYCATCHER and FLYCATCHER, respectively.

- The vultures found in Africa are a different family to the vultures found in North America. The African vultures' messages are listed under VULTURE, with the American vultures' listed under CONDOR.

- The magpies found in Great Britain and North America are a different family to the magpies found in Australia. Their messages are listed under MAGPIE and AUSTRALIAN MAGPIE, respectively.

- The dunnock of Great Britain is often known as a hedge sparrow, but it is not a sparrow. Its message is listed under DUNNOCK.

- The meadowlark of North America is not a lark; its message is listed under MEADOWLARK.

- In North America, the grosbeaks are members of either the bunting family or the finch family. The message of the cardinal, blue grosbeak and rose-breasted grosbeak is listed under BUNTING. The message of the evening grosbeak and pine grosbeak is listed under FINCH.

- All sparrows found in Great Britain, Australia and South Africa are of the weaver family and their message listed under WEAVER. All sparrows found in North America are of the bunting family and their message is listed under BUNTING (with the exception of the house sparrow, which is a member of the weaver family).

- The Northern flicker found in North America is a woodpecker and is listed under WOODPECKER.

So, if you are in North America and want to know the message of a song sparrow, look under BUNTING; if you want to know the message of the house sparrow, look under WEAVER.

It is no wonder that bird books adhere to the scientific names rather than the common names given to birds, because then there can be no mistaking which bird is which. However, to make life a little simpler and to assist you in finding the correct message for each bird, please use the Quick Reference Guide, found at the end of the Appendix.

Albatross
Message: **Intuition**   *Archetype:*   Intuitive
An albatross is saying you must start listening to your intuition and trust your instincts. Intuitive feelings are the way we receive guidance from our souls, spirit guides or angels. How many times have you had that "inner knowing" that it is time to move from the place you are living, or that your current job or romantic relationship is not right for you anymore, or that you should seek attention for a medical condition, or that you should enroll in an evening class or pursue a friendship or hobby. Are you listening to these intuitive hunches? What is stopping you from acting on your intuition?

Barbet
Message: **Routine**   *Archetype:*   Automaton
This African bird is saying you need more routine in your life, because your energies are scattered in too many directions and you are not focused. This may be in general or in one specific area of your life. Make a list of what needs to

be done, in priority order, then tick off what you have accomplished each day. Try to focus on one thing at a time so that you can concentrate your energies towards that goal alone. Alternatively, the barbet may be saying you adhere too much to a routine and that your life has become habitual and regimental, and you need to add some variety and be more flexible. Being too rigid and pre-programmed blocks the creative flow.

Blackbird, American *(incl. red-winged blackbird, yellow-headed blackbird, Brewer's blackbird)*

Message: **Courage**   *Archetype:*   Hero

American blackbirds are asking where in your life you need to have more courage. Are you able to step out boldly into the unknown and go after what you really want in life? Do you have the courage to confront obstacles in your life, or do you shy away from them? If you have firm ideas, do you have enough courage in your own convictions to stand up for your beliefs regardless of opposition? Conversely, are you rushing in where angels fear to tread, playing the hero because you want to prove your worth to yourself or to someone?

Bluebird

Message: **Love**   *Archetype:*   Lover

A bluebird is asking why are you afraid to love or be loved. Is it a fear of intimacy, of being hurt, rejected or betrayed? Love isn't just about giving – it is about receiving, too – but many people who are able to give love unfortunately close their heart when it comes to receiving it. Love is the highest vibration of all, and when you experience love, whether through another person, a pet, a painting or a sunset, you are experiencing Divine love. Alternatively, the bluebird may be telling you that you are so busy loving another person, whether they are present in your life or not, that it is taking your focus away from other areas of your life.

Bulbul

Message: **Ambition**   *Archetype:*   Goal Seeker

This African bird is saying you have lost your "get-up-and-go" and you are in a rut. You haven't any defined goals to strive for and, as a result, you feel apathetic and life has become dull and meaningless. Maybe you do have a dream or a goal, but your low self-esteem is making you believe it is unattainable. Decide on one realistic goal that is close to your heart, then set your intention to go after it. It does not matter how big or small the goal is, but when you make the decision to go after what you really want, then you will feel the motivation flood through you.

Bunting *(incl. cardinal, blue grosbeak, rose-breasted grosbeak, junco, yellowhammer, all American sparrows (except house sparrow))*

Message: **Humility**   *Archetype:* Mystic

Is there an area in your life where you are throwing your weight around and letting your ego think you know best? The bunting is saying, have enough humility to realize that you don't know all the answers, and that others also have talents and are entitled to their opinions, too. Can you perform a good deed without wanting the whole world to know about it? Are you angry because you are not getting enough recognition and praise for something, or have you been asked to do a task that you feel is beneath you? Maybe being asked to do a seemingly insignificant task is heaven's way of teaching you to have more humility. On the other hand, it could be that you are being too shy and modest about an accomplishment and not taking the credit that is due to you, and you are instead allowing your low self-esteem to get the applause.

Butcherbird, Australian

Message: **Venturousness**   *Archetype:* Gambler

This Australian bird is saying you need to be more adventurous in your life, to take the plunge and go after what it is you really want. Why are you waiting for things to happen instead of going after what you desire? Take a chance and strike out on the path you've always wanted to follow, and stop letting your fears hold you back. Nobody has ever achieved anything by sitting back and not taking a risk here and there. Alternatively, the butcherbird may be saying that you are a person who takes too many risks in life without heeding what the consequences may be.

Buzzard

Message: **Nourishment**   *Archetype:* Hedonist

A buzzard is asking you how you are nourishing your body. This isn't just in the food sense, but in other pleasures as well. Are you indulging yourself in ways that are healthy, or out of greed and selfishness? Do you make the time to pamper yourself or allow yourself to be pampered, or do you believe that this is narcissistic behavior? Are you able to attend to all your needs, or do you feel you do not matter? Your mind and soul need just as much nourishment as your physical body. Perhaps reading inspirational books and poetry, joining adult education classes, or starting yoga lessons or meditation classes appeals to you.

Canary

Message: **Companionship**   *Archetype:* Companion

When a canary appears, take a look at your social life and see whether you need to broaden your horizons. We shouldn't limit ourselves to just one friend or to one small group of people, because it is important to develop a broader social network of friends, separate from each other, so that each can provide support in the different areas of our lives. Alternatively, the canary may be saying you are keeping company with the wrong sort of people who are either not a good influence or are stopping you from moving forward. It could be that you have become too dependent on a friend, or they have become too dependent on you, in which case you need to re-evaluate the friendship and find out why this dependency has happened.

Catbird, Common

Message: **Detachment**   *Archetype:*   Vampire

Detachment means being able to do something, then detaching from the outcome. Do you always have firm ideas of how things are supposed to turn out, and when they don't go the way you want, do you become despondent and depressed? Maybe you try and take control of these situations and manipulate them to get the desired results? A catbird is saying, take a look at your life and see if there is an outcome to which you are attached, and if you are trying to control to get the results *you* want. Or are you attached to an object, a negative emotion or habit that doesn't serve a purpose in your life anymore? Maybe you are using manipulative means to keep a person attached to you.

Chicken

Message: **Patience**

A chicken is saying that there is a matter in your life where you need to exercise more patience. Are you waiting for something, and feeling angry and irritated that it hasn't arrived yet? Are you a person who always want things to happen when *you* want them to happen and you hate to be kept waiting? Alas, the heavens often find a way to make us wait for something, to help teach us patience. If you have an illness that seems to be dragging on and a chicken appears, it may mean that it is something you need to endure for a while, as it is part of your spiritual growth. Endurance may apply to other aspects of your life, too.

Condor *(All American vultures)*

Message: **Conquering**   *Archetype:*   Mountaineer

A condor is asking what in your life you need to conquer. Is it a bad habit, a fear? Why do you let it have power over you? Are you able to stand up to your adversaries or do you crumble and allow them to trample all over you? Do you have enough belief in yourself that you can overcome any obstacle put in your way, or do you throw in the towel at the first hurdle? The most powerful weapon you possess is your human spirit, which enables you to rise above and triumph over anything, so you can conquer new heights.

Coot

Message: **Discipline**   *Archetype:*   Drill Sergeant

A coot is saying there is an area in your life where more discipline is needed. Is it to do with a nutritional program or an exercise program you know you should adhere to, or is it to do with kicking a bad habit? Is your mind wandering here, there and everywhere when you sit and meditate? It takes hard work to be disciplined because it is a matter of training the mind in self-control. Alternatively, the coot may be saying you are a person who is too disciplined and that you run your life regimentally. Things might get done but you also put a lot of pressure on yourself. Or maybe you are too much of a disciplinarian with others, in which case you should release your control and give them the freedom to express themselves.

Cormorant

Message: **Independence** *Archetype:* Damsel

A cormorant is saying that you have become too dependent on something or someone. Maybe you are relying on another person to give you financial or emotional support that you do not believe you can give yourself. Are you able to stand up for yourself, or do you want others to protect you? You may have become dependent on an external substance. Conversely, are you a person who is too independent? Do you want to do everything yourself and not ask anybody for help? There are times when you cannot do everything, so either delegate the workload or ask for help. Asking for help is not a sign of weakness, but a mark of strength.

Coucal

Message: **Advice** *Archetype:* Adviser

This African bird is saying you need to get somebody else's opinion over a matter. More than likely, they will be able to give you recommendations and advice that you hadn't even thought of. Maybe you have a personal issue in your life that you are keeping to yourself. If this is the case the coucal is saying it is better that you talk it through with someone you trust, like a close friend, family member or even a counselor. Conversely, maybe someone came to you for advice and you didn't give them your honest opinion, for reasons known only to you. It could be the coucal is saying you have counseling abilities, which you should consider using.

Cowbird

Message: **Cooperation** *Archetype:* Team Player

A cowbird is saying there is an area in your life where teamwork is required. Maybe you want somebody else to do all the work, or you want to take sole charge and do it all by yourself. We all have different skills to offer, and maybe a project of some sort requires a combination of all the different expertise to bring it into fruition, with everybody pulling their weight. Similarly, there may be somebody close to you who wants to do something and you are standing in their way and not cooperating. Or do your spirit guides or angels want you to do something for your own spiritual growth but you are standing in your own way and not cooperating?

Crane

Message: **Contemplation** *Archetype:* Philosopher

A crane is telling you that you need to find some time alone in order to reflect on a certain area of your life where there may be a problem. You may want to incorporate prayer or meditation in this quiet time, but be sure you are able to be by yourself with no disturbances. You could sit in the garden or go to the local park if it helps, but it is important that you make this time for yourself in order to think things through and look within for answers. The crane may be telling you that it is time to incorporate a daily meditation practice into your life.

Crow
Message: **Change**   *Archetype:*   Shape-shifter
The appearance of a crow is saying that there is an area in your life where you need to make changes. Even the smallest change can create a big impact in your life. While birds are not fortune-tellers, a crow may be warning you that there will be changes coming into your life, but these changes will always be ultimately for your own benefit. Alternatively, the crow may be trying to make you aware that you are not being true to yourself because you keep changing your mind, ideas and beliefs depending on whom you are with at the time. Listen to what other people have to say but, at the end of the day, form your own beliefs that "feel right" for you and stick with them.

Cuckoo
Message: **Trust**
A cuckoo is saying that you need to trust more. This may mean having more trust and a firmer belief in your own abilities, having trust in another person with whom you are currently having dealings, trust that the outcome of a situation in your life will turn out the way it is supposed to, or have more trust in God. When something happens in your life and you don't know why, and a cuckoo appears at this time, it is telling you to trust that there is a higher reason for what is happening, according to a greater spiritual plan.

Cuckoo-shrike
Message: **Challenge**   *Archetype:*   Sentry
This Australian bird is saying there is a situation or problem in your life that you are not facing, and you're pretending it's not there. Denying the existence of a problem is not going to make it go away, and you need to confront it head on and deal with it. Have you been presented with some form of challenging work, and your self-doubt and lack of confidence are getting in the way? The cuckoo-shrike is saying, stop putting off the project, because you are more than capable to deal with the task at hand. Alternatively, are you unnecessarily challenging people and objecting to every idea they are putting forward? Is it because it makes you feel powerful and you get a kick out of being a disruptive force? The underlying reason is based on a fear, so turn your attention inwards and confront the fear instead.

Currawong
Message: **Abilities**   *Archetype:*   Pirate
This Australian bird is asking, are you using your talents, or do you fall into the trap of looking at successful people and thinking you could never do that because you do not have the capabilities? We all have a talent for something, so find what you are good at and put it to good use. When you are asked to do

something, do you put pressure on yourself by trying to do it perfectly, or do you go about it half-heartedly in a rush to get on to the next project? The currawong is saying that the only important thing is to strive to do things to the best of your ability. The currawong bird is a nest robber and is symbolically asking you whether you are able to use your own unique abilities, rather than stealing other people's.

Dove
Message: **Peace**
A dove is saying that you need to achieve peace of mind over a matter, or that peace of mind will come. If you are fretting over a situation and a dove appears, it is telling you to quieten your mind and to stop worrying, because dwelling on the problem is not only making the matter seem worse but it is stopping intuitive thoughts and guidance coming through. If you are currently going through a harrowing time, the appearance of a dove is reassuring you that peace is coming soon.

Duck
Message: **Faith**
Having complete faith in yourself, in God and in life itself is very easy when things are going well, but it is difficult to maintain when things are going wrong. Yet this is the time when it really counts. A duck is asking, where in your life is your sense of faith being challenged? Do you need to have more belief in yourself and your abilities? Or maybe you are being gently reminded that there is always divine and spiritual support. Developing a strong faith in the knowledge that God is always with you, that your angels and spirit guides are always there guiding and protecting you, and that you always have an endless source of inner strength waiting to be used, will give you the tools to overcome any problem. Faith is very powerful and can get you through any crisis.

Dunnock *(Also known as hedge sparrow)*
Message: **Determination**   *Archetype:*   Winner
A dunnock is asking what you want to accomplish, and whether you have the tenacity and drive to go after it. Where in your life do you need to make a firm decision about something, and then stick to it with a sense of purpose? When we procrastinate and put something off to a later date, we punish ourselves by adding more pressure and guilt for not having got it done, plus it stops the natural flow of things. Having the determination and resolve to do something in life means you have a good sense of self. Conversely, maybe you are persisting with something that is not meant to be a part of your life.

Eagle
Message: **Power and strength**   *Archetype:*   Leader
When an eagle appears, it is not telling you that you have to resort to brute force and muscle power to overcome an adversary, whether this is a person or a situation. Rather, it is encouraging you to use your innate *inner* power and

strength to rise above the problem, because only from this position are you able to see the bigger picture. Also, an eagle is asking you to look to see where in your life you are giving away your power to a problem or to another person. What underlying fear keeps you attached to the person or situation, either currently or in the past, which causes you to lose power? If you are involved in a power struggle with someone, do you have enough inner strength to walk away?

Emu
Message: **Fathering**   *Archetype:*   Father

Whether you are male or female, an emu is saying, look to see if you are being too dominant and overpowering over a family issue. Are you trying to exert your authority and ignoring the opinions of other family members? Maybe you are being too overprotective of your family and stifling them? If you are an employer with people working under you, the emu is saying you are being too aloof or domineering in the concerns of your employees, and you need to be more approachable. Alternatively, the emu may be telling you that you have the ability to be a guide and leader for other people in your field of interest.

Falcon
Message: **Loyalty**   *Archetype:*   Warrior

A falcon is prompting you to look at all areas of your life to see where you might not have been as loyal as you ought, and this includes being loyal to yourself. Can you be depended upon, or do you let people down? Do you fight other people's battles for them, or do you let them fight their own battles? Are you able to stand up for yourself and your beliefs, no matter who or what the adversaries? Did a friend tell you something in confidence that you gossiped to other people, or did you betray them in another way? Maybe you are the one who feels betrayed by someone. Can you be faithful and loyal without feeling duty-bound?

Finch *(incl. bullfinch, chaffinch, goldfinch, hawfinch, crossbill, evening grosbeak, pine grosbeak, redpoll)*
Message: **Compromise**   *Archetype:*   Prostitute

A finch is asking where in your life a compromise is needed. Is there a situation where you need to meet someone halfway? Life is a balance of give and take, but many people either give too much or take too much. Under which category do you fall? The finch may be telling you that you have put yourself in a compromising position in some way. Are you jeopardizing your own sense of integrity or your soul growth by allowing others to take advantage of you, or are you taking advantage of them? If you are praying to God for help with a matter, you must pull your weight and meet God halfway.

Flamingo

Message: **Balance**   *Archetype:* Juggler

A flamingo is asking, have you recently been upset when you didn't maintain your center? Did a person or situation throw you off balance and you got very hurt and angry instead of being poised and unfazed? Look at what negative beliefs the situation or the other person invoked in you, and use them as a learning curve. The flamingo may be telling you that you are in need of more balance in your life. It could be that you are focusing all your energies into one aspect of your life while neglecting other areas that also need your attention. Perhaps the flamingo is simply telling you that you need a more balanced diet.

Flycatcher, American (incl. peewee, phoebe, kingbird)

Message: Flow   *Archetype:* Mariner

We have all heard the expression, "go with the flow", and that is exactly what the American flycatcher is telling you to do. Where in your life are you standing still and refusing to move forward, even though every part of your being is urging you to move on? Are you able to forge ahead in uncharted waters, or does a fear of the future hold you back? When you stop moving, you literally stop the flow of new opportunities coming into your life. Alternatively, maybe you are drifting through life with no sense of purpose, in which case the American flycatcher is saying, set your horizons by deciding on a goal, and go after it.

Flycatcher (incl. Australian fantails and willie wagtail)

Message: **Dexterity**   *Archetype:* Engineer

The flycatcher is saying that you have a creative talent for something that requires using your hands, and now is the time to develop and use this skill. Whether you use this talent as a hobby or for monetary gain is up to you. It may be that you already know what this skill is and the flycatcher is saying that you need to become more masterful at it. Perhaps the flycatcher is telling you that you have a skill in handling matters, and that these managerial or mediation abilities are needed in some area of your life.

Goose

Message: **Truth**

A great many of our fears are based on perceptions that are seeded in childhood. Where in your life are you holding onto a perception instead of seeing what is the actual truth? Human beings love jumping to conclusions, looking at something based on assumptions rather than at the real truth of the matter. A goose is asking, where have you recently jumped to a conclusion without knowing all the facts and have subsequently made your life miserable? Alternatively, is there an area in your life where you haven't been truthful, either towards someone else or to yourself?

Grackle

Message: **Sociability**   *Archetype:*   Networker

Are you a naturally outgoing and approachable person? If so, are you using these qualities for everyone's benefit, or for selfish gains? Are you able to participate at social gatherings or do you sit in the corner and hope nobody notices you? Was there a time when you could have been a bit more neighbourly and friendly towards someone and, because you were not, it has left you feeling guilty? It could be that the grackle is telling you that you need to socialize more, to find friends or the fun times for which you've been longing. Alternatively, have you been putting too much emphasis on socializing, to the exclusion of other areas of your life?

Grouse

Message: **Contentment**   *Archetype:*   Monk/Nun

You may have a good job, sufficient money in the bank, and a meaningful relationship, but a grouse is asking, are you really contented? Are there still underlying fears that need to be addressed? Are you satisfied with what you already have in your life, or do you desire more? Do you worry that the things you do have will be taken away from you? God never intended for any of us to struggle and be miserable; that is merely what we have chosen for ourselves by holding onto negative beliefs.

Guinea Fowl

Message: **Stability**   *Archetype:*   Builder

A guinea fowl is asking what areas of your life are not built on solid ground and are, at best, a little bit shaky. Did you perhaps build a romantic partnership on a foundation of fears that is now beginning to crumble, or are you feeling insecure about the permanence of your job, a job that you originally built on the unfounded premise that the company would always provide for you? Are you relying on external support, like scaffolding, to hold you up, and if this scaffolding is taken away, will your whole world come crashing down? Stability begins with knowing you can support yourself, no matter what, and with knowing that your life should be built on a stable foundation of positive beliefs and faith.

Gull

Message: **Searching**   *Archetype:*   Explorer

A gull is asking what are you searching for in life. Is it happiness, success, wealth, love? What fears and negative beliefs have stopped you from finding what you're searching for? Have you been searching in the right places and with the right motives? Do you even know what it is you are after, or is it a bit vague and not well defined in your mind? Maybe you are on a quest to seek knowledge that can put you on a spiritual path, in which case you need to explore books and workshops to find the right tools with which to work and the right foundation to build on. If you are working toward something and you are not making much headway, the gull is saying, search out other ways of approaching the situation.

Hawk

Message: **Vigilance**   *Archetype:*   Lookout

A hawk is asking you to be alert and to keep your eyes open because there may be opportunities coming your way that you must grab. The hawk may be telling you that there is some area of your life where you need to view a situation with open eyes, instead of through rose-colored glasses as you have been doing. It could be that you are refusing to see a situation as it really is because you insist on fantasizing on a perfect ending. Perhaps the hawk is asking you to employ a "watch and wait" stance in some part of your life. It could be that you want to rush headlong into something without having all the facts, and this might not be the right time to "swoop in for the kill". In fact, the situation may pass over without any interference being necessary on your part.

Heron *(incl. egret)*

Message: **Solitude**   *Archetype:*   Hermit

A heron is saying you need to get away from other people for a while. We all have a need at some time in our lives to be by ourselves, and it is important for all of us to regularly take time out of our busy daily schedules to seek some solitude. These precious quiet times alone enable us to regain our energies and bearings, to reflect and ponder on private thoughts, or so that we can do what we want without worrying about other people. Maybe the opposite is true and you have isolated yourself from others, and now is the time to re-establish friendships or to pursue a social life.

Hoepoe

Message: **Vulnerability**   *Archetype:*   Sitting Duck

A hoepoe is asking, is there an area in your life where you feel vulnerable? If so, why do you feel threatened? Resilience comes from knowing your own inner strength and tapping into it. Conversely, are you a person who is as hard as nails on the surface but soft underneath? The hoepoe is saying, get rid of that suit of armor you have as an aura, and let your inherent gentler qualities come through. Letting this softer side show is not a sign of weakness. The hoepoe could also be warning you that your aura is energetically open, making you vulnerable to picking up harmful energies.

Honeyeater *(incl. miner)*

Message: **Kindness**   *Archetype:*   Samaritan

These Australian birds are asking, was there a recent incident where you may not have been tolerant and understanding towards someone? Did you speak too harshly because they caught you at a bad time, or was it that the problem or their attitude toward that problem mirror-imaged something in your own life that you are not facing? Maybe you haven't been as tolerant and kind to yourself recently. Conversely, the honeyeater may be telling you that you are giving too much kindness to somebody, and therefore keeping them stuck in their cycle of self-pity. Or have you been trying to offer unwanted kindly advice to someone and all you are doing is interfering in their life?

Hummingbird
Message: **Forgiveness**

A hummingbird appearing in your life is simply telling you that there is someone to forgive. This someone may be from your distant past, or currently in your life, but you are being urged to forgive them now because it is stopping you from moving forward in life. Holding grudges and resentments against people is a sure way to retard your spiritual growth, and while forgiving somebody seems a small task, it is in fact one of the most powerful things we can do for ourselves. True forgiveness has to be meaningful and has to come from your very heart and soul to have any real effect. It is also very important to forgive yourself, as well.

Ibis *(incl. hadeda ibis)*
Message: **Sensitivity**   *Archetype:*   Empath

An ibis is asking, are you oversensitive to other people's comments? Has there been a recent episode where you became upset by someone's actions or words towards you? Did this person really mean to hurt you, or did you just overreact? Are you sensitive to your own needs, and can you give yourself compassion when needed? Alternatively, the ibis may be saying you are being insensitive toward another person at a time when they need your understanding and support. Maybe this isn't an isolated incident, and you have permanently closed yourself off emotionally from other people as a way to prevent yourself from being hurt. The ibis may also be saying you need to be more sensitive to your own intuition.

Jay *(incl. blue jay)*
Message: **Opportunity**   *Archetype:*   Trickster

A jay may be telling you that an opportunity is going to present itself in a certain area of your life, so be ready. Sometimes the opportunities given to us are obvious, but many more come in subtle ways. Until we realize the many obscure ways opportunities can be presented to us, we are sometimes tricked into thinking that they are not really opportunities. Or maybe you do not grab opportunities because you do not want the extra responsibilities that often come with them. On the other hand, you may be an opportunist who sees opportunities in everything, even to the point of seeking them out. But are the opportunities there for the taking, or do you resort to underhanded methods of creating them at the expense of others?

Kingfisher *(incl. kookaburra)*
Message: **Relationships**   *Archetype:*   Shadow

A kingfisher is asking if there is an area in your life where you are having a problem relating to someone. Different people bring out the different facets of our personality and this is why other people are our greatest teachers. What annoys us most about another person is what is inherent but not acknowledged in ourselves. There is no spiritual law that says you have to like everybody. Try to understand the other person and see why they behave the way they do, and what fears are motivating them. You do not have to continue associating with this person if you don't want to, but you don't have to criticize them, either. The kingfisher is also asking you to look at your relationship with yourself, with your spirit guides and angels, and with God.

Kite

Message: **Focus**   *Archetype:* Marksman

A kite is saying that your energies are too scattered and you need to be more focused. Decide on one thing you want to achieve, and focus your attention on accomplishing it. Conversely, the kite may be telling you that you are focusing too much on your problems, which makes them appear worse than they really are. Dwelling on your fears and problems keeps you in their grip. Allow yourself a few minutes once a day to constructively ponder over your problem, then drop it from you mind for the rest of the day. In this way, you will be more open for the solution to flow into you.

Kiwi

Message: **Secretiveness**   *Archetype:* Clam

Do you always reply that everything is fine, even when it is not? Is this a form of denial? Do you have difficulty revealing your deepest feelings or valued opinions? There is nothing wrong with wanting others to respect your privacy, but by being so closed you are not giving others the chance to get to know the real and wonderful you. Conversely, do you have difficulty keeping secrets, so that when someone confides in you, you promptly feel the need to spread the information? The kiwi may appear to you at a time when you have been asked to keep a secret that has put you in a compromising position. Go to the person in question and tell them that you are no longer going to be a party to this type of information, and then completely remove yourself from the situation.

Lark

Message: **Healing**   *Archetype:* Healer

A lark is saying you need to heal old wounds before you can move forward in life. Are you still holding onto an emotional trauma from many years ago and, if so, are you not releasing it because you are still relishing the attention and pity it is giving you? Have you recently been through an emotional trauma but have not given yourself the time in which to heal? Maybe it is time to reconcile with someone that you have fallen out with, to put away your differences and renew the friendship. If you currently have a health problem, look to see what message the physical symptoms are giving you. Healing is not about being rid of physical symptoms; true healing takes place on the emotional, mental and spiritual levels, as well. The lark may be saying you have natural healing abilities and you should study one of the healing arts.

Loon

Message: **Expression**   *Archetype:*   Mime Artist

A loon is saying, take a look at the way you express yourself. This doesn't mean just verbal expression, but also the way you behave. Are you acting and dressing in ways that reflects your genuine self, or are you pretending to be something you are not, in a quest to fit in and impress? Why doesn't your sense of self-worth allow you the freedom to express yourself in any way you wish, with no apologies? Are you able to verbally express your needs, comfortably and with conviction, or do you get tongue-tied and embarrassed? Alternatively, the loon may be telling you that you have a talent that you are not using, through which you can express yourself.

Magpie

Message: **Inquisitiveness**   *Archetype:*   Detective

A magpie is saying you need to adopt a more enquiring mind and not be so resigned about your life by putting everything down to fate or "that's just the way life goes". In this age of becoming conscious, we have to switch to detective mode, probing into our own lives to discover our fears and negativities. Questioning our motives is a good place to begin. Are we motivated by our fears or from our hearts? What prompts us to make the choices we do? If you have come to a standstill over a problem, the magpie is saying you haven't dug deep enough and there are still answers to be found. On the other hand, the magpie may be saying you are a nosey-parker who wants to know everybody else's business. If this behaviour leads to envy, jealousy or bragging on your part, it only highlights your feelings of insecurity and inadequacy.

Magpie, Australian

Message: **Accommodation**   *Archetype:*   Innkeeper

This magpie is asking, are you able to accommodate new ideas, changes, or people into your life, or do you slam the door on them? Are you obliging when others ask for your assistance? Are you able to set aside a certain time for them and then get back to your own life, or are you over-accommodating and promptly take on all their problems? Do you go out of your way to impress people in order to fit in, or do you have a good sense of self-esteem and allow people to take you just the way you are? If there are upheavals in your life, the magpie is saying it is time that things are resolved once and for all so that you can get back to a settled environment.

Magpie-lark

Message: **Parenting**   *Archetype:*   Parent

This Australian bird is asking, are you still holding onto negative issues from your childhood concerning your parents and, if so, isn't it time to forgive and move on with your life? Maybe you have parenting issues with your own children that need addressing. It could be that you have forgotten to parent yourself by not attending to your own needs, or you have neglected the little child within. Maybe you are still acting like a child, wanting others to look after you and provide for all your needs. Or maybe you are insisting on parenting adults in your environment and not allowing them to grow up.

Meadowlark

Message: **Intention**

A meadowlark is saying it doesn't matter what you do in life, the most important thing is the intention behind it. Do you have intentions to get even with someone that you feel has wronged you? Or is your intention to forgive all those who have ever hurt you? Do you deliberately do things that you know are not beneficial to yourself or to others? Alternatively, do you have good intentions but never follow them through and put them into action? Maybe your intentions are not very clear in your mind, and you are faced with many paths in front of you and do not know which one to choose. Pray for guidance and chose a path that "feels right".

Mockingbird

Message: **Respect**   *Archetype:* Queen

A mockingbird is asking if you respect yourself. Do you treat yourself well emotionally, mentally and physically, or do you insist on punishing yourself? Are you considerate of other people? Do you respect their wishes, or do you try to control and dominate them so that they have to comply with your wishes? Do you have little regard for time, turning up late for appointments and being disrespectful of another person's time? Maybe you judge and criticize other people by their actions, but how do you know what the lessons are for another soul? Conversely, the mockingbird may be saying that it is one thing to admire and respect someone, but there's no need to put them on a pedestal. Or maybe you are the one who commands respect.

Moorhen (Gallinule)

Message: **Achievement**   *Archetype:* Achiever

A moorhen is asking, where in your life did you try to put a good idea into practice, only to abandon it because you thought it would fail or the idea was ridiculous? No idea is silly; if it were, you wouldn't have had it in the first place! Or maybe your low self-esteem persuaded you that you didn't have the necessary skills. Anything can be achieved if you really want it and you put your mind to it. Are you always starting something and not seeing it through to its completion, leaving a trail of unfinished projects behind? There is nothing wrong with having many projects on the go at the same time, but have more discipline to finish what you started, or you will never have a sense of achievement.

Mousebird

Message: **Prudence**   *Archetype:* Sage

This African bird is saying that careful thought is needed in some area of your life before you rush into things. It could be that you need to rethink the management of your finances and be more thrifty in your spending, or that you need to use your better judgment or more common sense over a matter. If you are faced with a decision, the mousebird is telling you to give it careful consideration, weighing up all the pros and cons, before you commit yourself to anything. On the other hand, the mousebird could be telling you that you want to start something but are being overcautious and therefore holding yourself back.

Nightingale
Message: **Hope**   *Archetype:*   Optimist

A nightingale is saying, no matter what is going on in your life right now, don't give up hope. There are times when we dearly hope for something to happen and it doesn't turn out the way we expected, but there is a difference between longing with a private agenda attached, and genuine hope that is infused with trust and faith. The way we want things to turn out is not always the way that God has planned, and expecting an outcome according to the way we want it to happen only sets us up for more despair. Things always turn out the way they are *supposed* to happen, according to a higher plan. Also bear in mind that sometimes we block a positive outcome by our negative beliefs.

Nightjar *(incl. nighthawk, whippoorwill, poorwill)*
Message: **Dreaming**   *Archetype:*   Visionary

A nightjar is asking you whether you are working towards your dreams and aspirations. What fears are stopping you from reaching for the stars? Do you even know what your dreams and aspirations are? On the other hand, are you wasting your days daydreaming and fantasizing about something or someone that is unrealistic or unobtainable? This wastes a lot of time, and the nightjar is urging you to pull away from these fantasies and to look for something real to strive for. The nightjar may also be alerting you to pay more attention to your dreams at night because there is guidance coming from that quarter.

Nuthatch
Message: **Decision-making**   *Archetype:*   Saboteur

If you are about to make an important decision and a nuthatch appears, it is asking you not to rush into things and to consider all sides of the story, as well as your motives. Maybe you are choosing to listen to your fears and incapacitating yourself from moving forward? Decision-making is an integral part of our daily lives, and no matter how big or small, decisions should all be analyzed from the perspective of the motivations behind the choices. This analysis into motives is an important step, particularly when you consider that with every decision comes the responsibility of the consequences of having made that decision.

Ostrich
Message: **Practicality**   *Archetype:*   Pragmatist

An ostrich is asking where in your life are you not being practical. Are your ideas about a situation impractical, are you acting unreasonably, or have you got unrealistic expectations about an outcome? Whatever the case, come back down to earth and review the situation from a more grounded level. Maybe you are spending your days daydreaming and fantasizing about the perfect mate, the perfect job, or the perfect house. Visualization must be done in a practical way; otherwise you will be lost in a dream world. Conversely, the ostrich could be telling you that you are being stubborn about an issue in your life where you have dug your heels into the ground and refused to budge.

Owl

Message: **Wisdom** *Archetype:* Wise Woman

An owl is telling you to use more wisdom in the decisions and choices you make. A wise move before you make any decision is to ask yourself your real motive for wanting to make that choice. Are you choosing to do something out of fear or out of wisdom? The owl is also asking you whether you are learning from your mistakes, or making the same mistakes over and over again. Are you reacting to a situation in the same negative way as you've always done, even when you know it is not working or helping? What are these situations trying to teach you? Learning by our mistakes makes us wiser. The owl is also reminding us how important it is to pass on any wisdom we have gained, because sharing what we have learned helps us all to grow.

Parrot

Message: **Communication** *Archetype:* Communicator

A parrot is asking, do you have communication skills that you are not using? This could be through the spoken or written word, but now is the time to see where these talents lie and to utilize them. Is there an area of your life where you are not speaking up for yourself, where you should be voicing your opinions in a constructive way instead of bottling them up inside? Conversely, the parrot may be warning you to think before you speak, and not to open your mouth and indiscriminately say things that you will later regret. Or perhaps you are gossiping behind people's backs? Does it make you feel powerful in some way, or are you doing it to fit in with the group?

Partridge

Message: **Commitment** *Archetype:* Knight

A partridge is asking, did you make a commitment to do something and you didn't follow through with your promise? When you break a promise, you are actually dishonoring yourself. Maybe you keep committing yourself to things you really don't want to do, saying yes to people when you should have said no. Are you able to commit yourself to one thing and see it through to its completion? Alternatively, are you devotedly committed to a cause or a person, and neglecting your own needs or the needs of others close to you? Maybe you have become too duty-bound over something that doesn't concern you, and have put unnecessary burdens on yourself.

Peacock

Message: **Honesty**   *Archetype:*   Politician

A peacock is asking where in your life you are not being completely honest and open. Is this towards another person, or with yourself? Are you not being open and honest with another person because you are worried about what they will say or think? Or maybe you are fooling yourself that something in your life is working well when in fact it's not? Were you dishonest or unethical at some time in your life and your conscience is still pricking you? If so, look to see what prompted you to act dishonestly, acknowledge it, forgive yourself and learn from the experience so that you can be free from that burden.

Pelican

Message: **Adaptability**   *Archetype:*   Contortionist

Can you go anywhere at any time, at a moment's notice, or do you need prior warning so that you have time to prepare? A pelican is saying that occasionally doing things spontaneously is actually great fun, and your whole world will not fall apart for having been a bit rash. Being rigid greatly limits your enjoyment of life. Are you able to adjust to changes in your life and adapt to new people or situations, and if not, what fears hold you back? The pelican may also be telling you that there is an area in your life where you need to be more flexible because you are blocking your natural creative flow by rigidly sticking to working only one way.

Penguin

Message: **Responsibility**   *Archetype:*   Adult

A penguin is asking, is there an area in your life where you need to be more responsible? Are you a reliable and responsible person, someone who can be counted on, or is there a part of you that is frightened to grow up and take the responsibilities of being an adult? Are you able to take responsibility for your thoughts and actions? On the other hand, the penguin may be telling you that you are taking on too much responsibility in some area of your life. Perhaps these responsibilities are not directly related to you, but you have taken them on anyway because of your inability to say no. Or is it because you feel duty-bound, or have difficulty delegating work, or that you want to impress someone?

Pheasant

Message: **Fairness**   *Archetype:*   Judge

Do you complain that life is not fair, that nothing ever goes right, or that you never get what you want? Are you very critical of yourself and of others, and you always strive for perfection in whatever you do? The pheasant is asking you to stop judging the world and God, and comparing yourself with others. Rather, look inwards at your own limiting beliefs, and focus on what you can create instead of what you don't have. On the other hand, the pheasant may be telling you that you have the ability to be a mediator because you are able to see both sides of an issue in an unbiased way, or that you have good judgment, such as being a good judge of character.

Pigeon

Message: **Obedience**   *Archetype:*   Rebel

Do you feel you have to conform to social norms and behave in ways that society expects of you? Are you controlled by outside influences? Maybe you are someone who does things exactly the way others tell you to do them. The pigeon is saying that, while abiding by the laws of the land is obviously important, you are under no social pressure about how to live your life. Listen to advice, make up your own mind, and strike out on a path of your own. Maybe you feel tied down and duty-bound by someone or something. Is it of your own doing? On the other hand, do you deliberately rebel because you want to be noticed and to fit in, or do you genuinely have a sense of your own worth?

Plover *(incl. killdeer, lapwing)*

Message: **Guidance**   *Archetype:*   Guide

A plover is reminding you that you are always being guided from the spirit realm. Are you listening to this guidance? Have you been getting a "hunch" or a "knowing" that you should or shouldn't do something, and you are not following it through? We expect guidance to be profound with cut and dry answers but, for the most part, it comes to us in subtle ways. When you pray for guidance, don't force the answers but know they will come, usually when you least expect them. The plover may also be telling you that you need to approach someone on the physical plane – a best friend or a counselor – for guidance over a matter.

Puffin

Message: **Genuineness**   *Archetype:*   Clown

A puffin is saying that, no matter who or what you are, it is important never to lose your identity and always to be yourself. Are you putting on a different mask depending on whom you are with at the time? The problem with putting on an act is that you have to keep it up, and the mask can be knocked off at any time, leaving you exposed. The irony is that the person whom you are trying to impress intuitively senses that you are not being yourself, and if they are ever given the chance to get to know the "real" you, they are much happier and at ease than when they have to deal with the "pretend" you.

Quail *(incl. bobwhite)*

Message: **Innocence**   *Archetype:*   Fool

Do you complain because you feel you always get blamed for things when it is not your fault? The quail is saying maybe you have an underlying need to feel punished and put upon, and so fool yourself and others about your innocence. Is there an area in your life where you feel guilty? Guilt stems either from something you felt you should have done but didn't, or something you did and wish you hadn't. Did you act out of ignorance because you didn't know any better at the time, or were you fully aware of your motives? Alternatively, the quail may be telling you that you are being too gullible or naive over a matter in your life, and you need to look at things a little more seriously. Or maybe you are being asked to stop making life so complicated, and to look at things from a simpler perspective and a more worldly view.

Raven

Message: **Knowledge**   *Archetype:* Student

Do you feel better than other people because you possess certain knowledge, or is the opposite true and you feel worthless because you do not feel as smart as other people? Do you share the knowledge that you have gained? If you are faced with something, whether it is an illness or going into a new venture, the raven is saying to read all you can on the matter so that you can have a clearer understanding to help you with any future choices and decisions that are to be made. The raven is also saying that, while there is nothing wrong with acquiring a vast amount of knowledge, it is important to put this knowledge into practice. Being the perpetual student and learning for the sake of learning is not going to get you far where your soul growth is concerned, because you need to learn by experience as well.

Robin *(All robins of the Turdidae family)*

Message: **Protection**   *Archetype:* Guardian

A robin is asking, do you still look to other people to protect you and look after you, just as a child looks to an adult for protection? Or are you being overprotective towards someone? The robin may be saying there is an aspect in your life where you need to protect your interests or your reputation. Are you sure you are dealing with reputable companies or individuals? Or are you threatening your own credibility by doing something that you know in your heart you should not be doing? The robin may also be alerting you to the fact that you are not energetically protecting yourself as well as you might, and you are letting others sap your energies.

Shrike *(incl. bokmakerie)*

Message: **Sacrifice**   *Archetype:* Martyr

A shrike is asking, what do you need to let go of that is hampering your soul's growth? Is it a bad habit, a negative belief, or a relationship that has come to an end? It is a sacrifice in our eyes because the fearful side of us doesn't want to let go, yet we know we must let go if we want to continue on our spiritual journey. Do you complain that nobody appreciates you or notices what you have done for them, or that you are always blamed for something when it is not your fault? Why do you enjoy feeling martyred in this way? Have you had a worrying problem that you've given over to God in your prayers, only to snatch it back the next day? The ultimate act of sacrifice is the surrender of our will to the will of God – to live our lives wholly and completely by Divine wisdom.

Shrike-thrush

Message: **Uniqueness**   *Archetype:*   God/Goddess

We are all unique individuals with our own unique talents and ways of doing things. These Australian birds are telling you to stop following in the footsteps of others, because you have the ability to forge your own path. Learn the basic techniques to give you the foundation, and then build on this foundation in your own unique way. It could be that your unique style is needed in a project, so step forward and offer your services. On the other hand, the shrike-thrush may be telling you that you have isolated yourself, either physically or by not sharing your ideas, opinions and talents with others, and now is the time to be more visible so that others can benefit from your uniqueness.

Starling *(incl. mynah)*

Message: **Confidence**

A starling is asking in which area of your life you need to have more confidence. Where are you holding yourself back and stopping yourself from moving forward by a lack of belief in your talents and capabilities? Perhaps there is a current issue in your life that the starling is telling you to approach with more confidence. Or maybe there is a certain matter that is worrying you that you are keeping to yourself, and the starling is prompting you to find someone with whom you can talk it over in confidence. Conversely, are you a person who is walking around with an apparent air of confidence but deep down you have feelings of inadequacy? Work at building true self-confidence that can never be taken away from you.

Stork

Message: **Creativity**   *Archetype:*   Co-creator

Being creative literally means "bringing into being". We create our lives and everything in them, so when a stork appears, look at the different aspects of your life and ask yourself whether you like everything that is there. In the areas that you are not happy with, find out what negative beliefs you are using to do the creating. The stork may be telling you that you have a talent in the creative arts and now is the time to start using these abilities. If you have good ideas in your mind, now is the time to give birth to them and bring them into physical reality.

Sunbird

Message: **Joy and happiness**

A sunbird is saying that you need to find more joy and happiness in your life. Are you insisting on seeing life through the lens of struggle, refusing to let go of self-pity and feeling victimized? Or are you stopping joy and happiness from entering certain areas of your life by having limiting beliefs like, "I'll only be happy when I have money (or love, or health)". Beliefs like that only hold money, love or health at bay, so why not be happy now, so that when you do drop the limiting beliefs and allow these things to flow into your life, they can enhance the joy and happiness that is already there? If you have been going through a bad patch or have been feeling a little low, the sunbird is telling you that joy and happiness will be coming your way soon.

Swallow *(incl. martin)*

Message: **Acceptance**   *Archetype:*   Recipient

The swallow is asking, are you able to gratefully accept things given to you, whether in the form of assistance, a gift or a compliment, or do you get angry, embarrassed or uncomfortable? Maybe you are doing things to please other people, as a way to be accepted. Are you always taking on other people's problems when they do not really concern you, or are you accepting verbal or physical abuse and doing nothing about it? Are you accepting things as they really are, or are you in a form of denial? Acceptance is also the last of five stages of healing, following denial, anger, bargaining and depression. Every stage of the healing process is very important, but once you truly accept the problem, you automatically stop resisting the flow of healing energies.

Swan

Message: **Transformation**   *Archetype:*   Alchemist

When a swan appears, look to see what changes you can make in order to create wonderful transformations in your life. What negative beliefs can you convert into positive ones? What dominating fears can you use to motivate you into action rather than letting them depress you? Mastering fears and negative beliefs can produce marvelous, life-altering changes in your life. The swan may be telling you that it is time for a radical change on the physical plane – a new hairstyle, a change in dress style or make-up, or even a change in home or country, any of which will change your energy vibrations and literally give you a new lease on life. Everything in life is made up of energies, and energy cannot be destroyed; it can only be transformed.

Swift

Message: **Freedom**   *Archetype:*   Liberator

A swift is asking where in your life you feel trapped. Is it in a job you do not like, or in a relationship? Are you keeping yourself chained to events and people in the past and refusing to forgive and let go, or are you keeping yourself in bondage by your fears and negative beliefs? If you have spent years being dictated to by others, the swift is saying that it is now time for you to find autonomy and independence. We are our own jailer and liberator. On the other hand, the swift may be saying you have given someone too much free rein and you need to exercise firmer restraint with them. Or maybe you need free time to yourself, away from the daily schedules and crowds.

Thrasher

Message: **Necessity**

A thrasher is asking you to look at your life to see how many choices you are making out of a feeling of necessity. Are you doing things that you feel you *ought* to do, just to please your parents or your mate, or because society says you should do it that way? What are you doing in life that *you* really want to do, regardless of what anybody else says or thinks? Conversely, the thrasher may be telling you that there is something important you need to do but you are deliberately busying yourself with lots of trivial and unnecessary things as a way to avoid addressing the important issue.

Thrush *(incl. European blackbird)*
Message: **Nurturing/caring**   *Archetype:*   Mother

A thrush is saying that it is time you gave yourself some tender, loving care ,because you have been so busy catering to other people's needs that you have forgotten about yourself. Allow yourself some quality time and treat yourself to that facial, pedicure or massage. It could be that you are not caring for yourself in a healthy way, and now is the time to re-evaluate how you are nurturing your physical body, your mind and your soul. The thrush may be telling you that you are mothering somebody (a friend, mate or child) and it is time to let go and let them stand on their own two feet. Maybe you still have issues with your mother that need to be resolved.

Titmouse *(incl. blue tit, coal tit, great tit, chickadee)*
Message: **Resourcefulness**   *Archetype:*   Innovator

If you are faced with a problem and can't seem to find a way out, the titmouse is saying you are not using all your resources. Solving a problem sometimes takes a little inventiveness and imagination. Your soul knows the answers to all problems and will guide you to where the answers may be found. Resources can come in the form of your own intellect, from books, workshops, talking things over with a friend, meditation, or financial aid. The titmouse may be telling you that you possess a talent that you are not using, or it could be that you have exhausted all your resources and it is time to learn new skills to enable you to move on to other arenas.

Toucan
Message: **Boundaries**   *Archetype:*   Victim

A toucan is asking you to look at the personal boundaries you have set. Do you allow people to invade your space or infringe upon your rights, either physically, emotionally or mentally, because you are afraid that if you say no then nobody will like you or you will feel unwanted? Have you given others the right to be in charge of your life, allowing them to make decisions for you, or are you allowing other people's self-pity routines to keep you at their beck and call? Maybe you are the one who is manipulating and controlling others. Conversely, the toucan may be saying that you have walled yourself off from the rest of the world, not allowing anybody in. Taking down the wall doesn't have to leave you feeling vulnerable, because you then set your boundaries by being selective of whom, or what, you are going to allow into your space.

Turaco *(incl. lourie, go-away bird, plantain-eater)*

Message: **Preservation**   *Archetype:* Environmentalist

These birds are asking how you preserve yourself in life. Are you able to maintain a healthy personal environment that includes both the internal environment of your body and mind as well as your external environment? Where in your life do you feel hemmed in? Or maybe you like to be enclosed by routine and external support systems as a way to feel safe and secure. Is there an area of your life where you are not safeguarding your personal boundaries? Do you amass junk in your home because of sentimental reasons, or because it might come in handy one day? What are the underlying reasons for your hanging onto such things?

Turkey

Message: **Abundance**   *Archetype:* Midas

The word "abundance" is often taken to mean having lots of money. In fact, it means having an abundance of health, love, joy, peace and success, as well. A turkey is saying, look at your life and see what is lacking and where. Maybe you are concentrating all your efforts on attaining abundance in one area of your life, to the exclusion of other areas? Are you happy in your career but not in your home life, or successful in love but struggling financially? What are the fears and negative beliefs that have stopped you from having abundance in all areas of your life? We are entitled to abundance in every way, but life is also about balance. The turkey is also reminding you to be thankful for what you do have.

Vireo

Message: **Deserving**   *Archetype:* Ascetic

Do you keep yourself from having wonderful things happening in your life because of an inner belief that you don't really deserve them? Do you feel you're not good enough, clever enough or attractive enough to have the things you want in life? Do you deny yourself having love or money, for example, because you feel you need to be punished in some way, or do you believe that good things happen to other people and you're not one of the lucky ones? The vireo is saying, stop justifying your lack of success by making unfounded excuses, and deal with your limiting beliefs, because we are all entitled to wonderful things in life.

Vulture

Message: **Death/rebirth**

A vulture does not represent physical death. Rather, the message is of a complete ending of a situation, whether it be a relationship, an illness, a job, a place of residence, a cycle of events, a habit, or an old way of thinking – and this clears the way for a fresh start. On what chapter in your life have you not closed the door? Who or what is keeping you chained to the past so that the new beginnings that are in store for you, cannot come into play? Rebirth always follows death, but there can be no rebirth without death of the old.

Wagtail

Message: **Harmony**   *Archetype:* Arbitrator

The wagtail is asking where in your life there is disharmony or chaos. Energies should flow harmoniously through every aspect of your life; if they are not flowing, find out what is causing them to dam up. If you are angry or in a disagreement with someone, the wagtail is saying it is time to resolve the issue amicably instead of harboring grudges. Are you not cooperating with others over a project, and thus slowing down the process and causing disruptions? Or maybe you are being asked to act as a go-between to bring harmony between two warring parties.

Warbler, American *(incl. ovenbird, yellowthroat, kinglet)*

Message: **Gratitude**

When an American warbler appears, ask yourself if you are grateful for what you have in your life. Usually we are so busy complaining about what is not working in our lives and what we have not got, that we forget to be thankful for what we do have. It is particularly cathartic at those times when nothing seems to be going right, to mentally list and appreciate the things with which you are already blessed; it will change your perception. No matter how bad your life appears, there is *always* something to be grateful for. Maybe you were ungrateful towards someone who gave you something, instead of being thankful.

Warbler

Message: **Request**   *Archetype:* Beggar

A warbler is asking, is there an area of your life where you want to ask someone for something but you are too frightened to ask in case the answer is no? Is it because this other person intimidates you, or because your low self-esteem will generate a negative answer? Do you always feel you have to ask for permission to do something, particularly from a spouse or mate? Maybe you rely on other people to take care of you and all your needs. On the other hand, are you there for others when they ask for assistance, or do you forget about their problems because your life is going so well? When you pray to God for guidance, do you ask for help, or do you beg for it?

Waxwing

Message: **Objectivity**   *Archetype:* Observer

A waxwing is saying that in some area of your life you need to look at things more objectively. Maybe your emotions are getting in the way so that you cannot see the whole picture clearly. If so, step out of the frame and view the situation from the outside to help clarify things, and you will probably find you have been getting yourself upset over assumptions rather than seeing what is real. Similarly, the waxwing may be telling you to be more open-minded about an issue in your life because you are stubbornly refusing to see all sides of the story. On the other hand, it may be that you are being too disinterested towards a person or a subject which needs your full attention and cooperation.

Weaver *(incl. house sparrow, tree sparrow, cape sparrow, quelea)*
Message: **Consolidation**   *Archetype:*   Weaver
A weaver is asking, is there an area in your life where things are not quite coming together? Maybe you need to unite the people around you so that you can all work as a team to get something accomplished. Or maybe you need to incorporate new ideas, or merge already existing ideas into one good plan. It could be that your thoughts are too scattered and need to be consolidated towards one main objective. Perhaps there may be loose ends that need to be tied up before you can move on to a new project or a new phase in your life. Who in your life is spinning you a yarn which you have fallen for, or are you the one who is fabricating facts?

White-eye
Message: **Perserverance**   *Archetype:*   Researcher
A white-eye is saying you need to be more persistent in some area of your life. Do you have good ideas but are not following them through and putting them into action? If there is an area in your life where you are beginning to waver because things either look difficult or are becoming tedious, the white-eye is saying, stay with it and persevere because you will be amazed at your accomplishments and the results. Conversely, the white-eye may be telling you that you are insisting on chasing after pipe dreams and fantasies that are just not meant to be.

Woodpecker *(incl. flicker, American yellowhammer)*
Message: **Security**   *Archetype:*   Child
Do you have an underlying feeling of apprehension that the whole world is an unsafe place in which to live and that there is danger lurking on every corner? Are you refusing to move forward in life because you are afraid of the unknown, and you'll only move forward if you can be guaranteed a positive and safe outcome? Maybe you are relying on outside sources, like a healthy bank balance, to make you feel secure, or you are relying on another person to provide security for you. The woodpecker is asking you to understand that these issues of insecurity are only based on perceptions and that you are more than capable of creating your own sense of security. All that's needed to take a step into the unknown is the faith of a child and the convictions of an adult.

Wren
Message: **Self-worth**
A wren is asking how you value yourself. Are you worth a lot in your own eyes, or do you think of yourself as insignificant and meaningless? Are you easily influenced by other people's opinions, and bow down as soon as there is a hint of opposition, or are you able to stand up and voice your own beliefs? Where in your life are you holding yourself back by deliberately not starting projects because you think you are not good enough? Do you deny yourself all the wonderful things life has to offer because you think you do not deserve them?

We are all made from Divine essence, and not feeling worthy is like saying you do not care much about the stock you came from!

Wren-warbler *(incl. fairy-wren, brown thornbill)*

Message: **Imagination**   *Archetype:*   Artist

The Australian wren-warbler is asking, are you able to use your imagination in a positive, constructive way, or do you run everything by your fears and imagine the worst will happen in every situation? Do you have the courage to go ahead with fanciful ideas as a way to express yourself, or do you feel you should stick with the mundane? The wren-warblers may be telling you that you have a good imagination and you should consider channeling it into something creative, like writing, music, or some other artistic endeavor. If you are faced with a problem, you are being asked to use a little ingenuity; this coupled with visualizing a positive outcome will go a long way in helping you to solve it.

Quick Reference Guide

Bird	Message	Archetype
Albatross	Intuition	Intuitive
Barbet	Routine	Automaton
Blackbird, American	Courage	Hero
Blackbird, European	(*See* Thrush)	
Bluebird	Love	Lover
Blue Grosbeak	(*See* Bunting)	
Blue Jay	(*See* Jay)	
Blue Tit	(*See* Titmouse)	
Bobwhite	(*See* Quail)	
Bokmakerie	(*See* Shrike)	
Bulbul	Ambition	Goal Seeker
Bunting	Humility	Mystic
Butcherbird, Australian	Venturousness	Gambler
Buzzard	Nourishment	Hedonist
Canary	Companionship	Companion
Cardinal	(*See* Bunting)	
Catbird, Common	Detachment	Vampire
Chickadee	(*See* Titmouse)	
Chicken	Patience	
Condor	Conquering	Mountaineer
Coot	Discipline	Drill Sergeant
Cormorant	Independence	Damsel
Coucal	Advice	Adviser
Cowbird	Cooperation	Team Player
Crane	Contemplation	Philosopher
Crow	Change	Shape Shifter
Cuckoo	Trust	
Cuckoo-shrike	Challenge	Sentry
Currawong	Abilities	Pirate
Dove	Peace	
Duck	Faith	
Dunnock	Determination	Winner

Bird	Message	Archetype
Eagle	Power and Strength	Leader
Egret	(*See* Heron)	
Emu	Fathering	Father
Evening Grosbeak	(*See* Finch)	
Falcon	Loyalty	Warrior
Fantail, Australian	(*See* Flycatcher)	
Finch	Compromise	Prostitute
Flamingo	Balance	Juggler
Flicker	(*See* Woodpecker)	
Flycatcher, American	Flow	Mariner
Flycatcher	Dexterity	Engineer
Gallinule	(*See* Moorhen)	
Goose	Truth	
Grackle	Sociability	Networker
Grouse	Contentment	Monk/Nun
Guinea Fowl	Stability	Builder
Gull	Searching	Explorer
Hadeda	(*See* Ibis)	
Hawk	Vigilance	Lookout
Hedge Sparrow	(*See* Dunnock)	
Heron	Solitude	Hermit
Hoepoe	Vulnerablility	Sitting Duck
Honeyeater	Kindness	Samaritan
House Sparrow	(*See* Weaver)	
Hummingbird	Forgiveness	
Ibis	Sensitivity	Empath
Jay	Opportunity	Trickster
Junco	(*See* Bunting)	
Killdeer	(*See* Plover)	
Kingfisher	Relationships	Shadow
Kinglet	(*See* Warbler)	
Kite	Focus	Marksman
Kiwi	Secretiveness	Clam
Kookabura	(*See* Kingfisher)	
Lark	Healing	Healer
Loon	Expression	Mime Artist
Lourie	(*See* Turaco)	

Bird	Message	Archetype
Magpie	Inquisitiveness	Detective
Magpie, Australian	Accommodation	Innkeeper
Magpie-lark	Parenting	Parent
Martin	(*See* Swallow)	
Meadowlark	Intention	
Miner	(*See* Honeyeater)	
Mockingbird	Respect	Queen
Moorhen	Achievement	Achiever
Mousebird	Prudence	Sage
Mynah	(*See* Starling)	
Nighthawk	(*See* Nightjar)	
Nightingale	Hope	Optimist
Nightjar	Dreaming	Visionary
Nuthatch	Decision-making	Saboteur
Ostrich	Practicality	Pragmatist
Owl	Wisdom	Wise Woman
Parrot	Communication	Communicator
Partridge	Commitment	Knight
Peacock	Honesty	Politician
Pelican	Adaptability	Contortionist
Penguin	Responsibility.	Adult
Pheasant	Fairness	Judge
Pigeon	Obedience	Rebel
Plover	Guidance	Guide
Puffin	Genuineness	Clown
Quail	Innocence	Fool
Raven	Knowledge	Student
Redpoll	(*See* Finch)	
Robin	Protection.	Guardian
Rose-breasted Grosbeak	(*See* Bunting)	
Shrike	Sacrifice	Martyr
Shrike-thrush	Uniqueness	God/Goddess
Sparrow, American	(*See* Bunting)	
Sparrow (House and Tree)	(*See* Weaver)	
Starling	Confidence	
Stork	Creativity	Co-creator
Sunbird	Joy and Happiness	
Swallow	Acceptance	Recipient

Bird	Message	Archetype
Swan	Transformation	Alchemist
Swift	Freedom	Liberator
Thornbill, brown	(*See* Wren-warbler)	
Thrasher	Necessity	
Thrush	Nurturing/Caring	Mother
Titmouse	Resourcefulness	Innovator
Toucan	Boundaries	Victim
Tree Sparrow	(*See* Weaver)	
Turaco	Preserving	Environmentalist
Turkey	Abundance	Midas
Vireo	Deserving	Ascetic
Vulture, American	(*See* Condor)	
Vulture	Death/Rebirth	
Wagtail	Harmony	Arbitrator
Warbler, American	Gratitude	
Warbler	Request	Beggar
Waxwing	Objectivity	Observer
Weaver	Consolidating	Weaver
Whipoorwill	(*See* Nightjar)	
White-eye	Perseverance	
Willie Wagtail, Australian	(*See* Flycatcher)	
Woodpecker	Security	Child
Wren	Self-worth	
Wren-warbler	Imagination	Artist
Yellowhammer, American	(*See* Woodpecker)	
Yellowhammer, European	(*See* Bunting)	
Yellowthroat	(*See* Warbler, American)	

Notes

Chapter One ~ Feathered Friends

1. *The Reader's Digest Illustrated Guide to Southern Africa.* (1985). Cape Town: The Reader's Digest Association South Africa Pty Ltd. p. 272

2. *Ibid.*

Chapter Two ~ Spiritual Communicators

1. Rothschild, Joel. (2001). *Signals: An Inspiring Story of Life After Life.* London: Bantam Press.

Chapter Three ~ Link with the Divine

1. Robinson, Lytle. (1976). *Edgar Cayce's Story of the Origin and Destiny of Man.* New York: The Berkley Publishing Group. Chap. 2

2. Cooper, Diana. (1996). *A Little Light On Angels.* Scotland: Findhorn Press. p.11

3. *Ibid.* Chaps. 20, 21, 25

4. Bailey, A. Alice. (1951). *A Treatise of Cosmic Fire.* New York: Lucis Publishing Company. pp.895–6

5. *Ibid.*

6. Wall, Vicky. (1991). *The Miracle of Colour Healing.* London: The Aquarian Press. Excerpt taken from chap. 17, "The Chakras"

7. Cooper, Diana. (2001). *Angel Inspiration.* London: Hodder and Stoughton. Chap. 5

Chapter Four ~ Birds in Mythology

1. Jung, Carl. (1998). *Man and His Symbols.* London: Picador. pt.1

2. *Ibid.,* pp. 41, 57

3. For a comprehensive account of archetypes, and of how to work with them in your life, please see Caroline Myss' *Sacred Contracts* (New York: Harmony Books, 2001).

4. Melchizedek, Drunvalo. (1998). *The Ancient Secret of the Flower of Life.* Flagstaff, Arizona: Light Technology Publishing. Vol. 1, pp. 118, 127

5. Marie-Louise von Franz, in Carl Jung et al., *Man and His Symbols.* p. 220

6. Joseph L. Henderson, in Carl Jung et al., *Man and His Symbols.* p. 153

7. *Ibid.*

8. Timms, Moira. (1994). *Beyond Prophecies and Predictions.* New York: Ballantine Books. p. 51–52

9. *Ibid.*

10. Melchizedek, *The Ancient Secret of the Flower of Life.* Vol. 1, p. 131

11. Timms, *Beyond Prophecies and Predictions.* p. 219

12. *Ibid.*, pp. 47, 220

Chapter Six ~ How Birds have Helped Humanity

1. Perrins, Dr. Christopher, & Harrison, Dr. C.J.O. (1979). *Birds: Their Life, Their Ways, Their World.* New York: The Reader's Digest Association Inc. p. 134

2. *Ibid.*, p. 139

3. Edgar Cayce Australia. (n.d.). *Pineal Gland.* Available from: http://www.cayce.egympie.com.au?healthpinealgland.htm

Chapter Seven ~ Feathers

1. Leofwine & Yffi. (2002). *Quills – Part 2: Cutting a Quill Pen.* Regia Anglorum Publications. Available: http://www.regia.org/quill2.htm

2. Fletcher, Alan. (2001). *The Art of Looking Sideways.* London: Phaidon Press Ltd. p. 63

3. Gerber, Richard. (1993). *Vibrational Medicine.* Vermont: Bear & Company. p. 225

4. Andrews, Ted. (1993). *Animal Speak: The Spiritual & Magical Powers of Creatures Great & Small.* Minnesota: Llewellyn Publications. p. 69

Chapter Eight ~ Eggs

1. Perrins, Dr. Christopher, & Harrison, Dr. C.J.O. (1979). *Birds: Their Life, Their Ways, Their World.* New York: The Reader's Digest Association Inc. pp. 119–20

2. Lazaris. *Giving Voice To Your Soul.* On Cassette tape. Lazaris is the spirit guide who channels through Jach Pursel. For more information on the works of Lazaris, call or write to Concept Synergy, 1-800/678-2356, PO Box 3285, Palm Beach, Florida, 33480

3. Eden, Donna. (1998). *Energy Medicine.* New York: Jeremy P Tarcher/ Putnam. p. 119

4. Shine, Betty. (1990). *Mind To Mind.* London: Corgi Books. pp. 242–3

Chapter Ten ~ Putting the Messages to Practical Use

1. Dee, Nerys. (1984). *Your Dreams and What They Mean.* Northamptonshire: The Aquarian Press.

Bibliography

Ambrose-Bates, Linda. (n.d.). *Churchill's Pet Unmasked.* Available from: http://www.pet-manual.co.uk/showthread/t-12787.html .

Ames, Delano. (Ed.). (1963). *Greek Mythology.* London: Paul Hamlyn Ltd.

Andrews, Ted. (1998). *Animal Speak: The Spiritual and Magical Powers of Creatures Great and Small.* Minnesota: Llewellyn Publications.

Andrews, Ted. (1999). *Animal- Wise: The Spirit Language and Signs of Nature.* Jackson: Dragonhawk Publishing.

Bailey, A. Alice. (1951). *A Treatise of Cosmic Fire.* New York: Lucis Publishing Company.

Bailey, A. Alice. (1962). *Esoteric Psychology: Vol. 1. A Treatise on the Seven Rays.* New York: Lucis Publishing Company.

Bauval, Robert, & Hancock, Graham. (1996). *Keeper of Genesis: A Quest For the Hidden Legacy of Mankind.* London: William Heinemann Ltd.

The Birdman of Alcatraz: A Brief Narrative on Robert Shroud. (n.d.). Available from: http://www.alcatrazhistory.com/stroud.htm .

Bird Folklore. (n.d.). Mystical World Wide Web. Available from: http://www.mystical-www.co.uk/birds.htm .

Christie, Anthony. (1968). *Chinese Mythology.* London: The Hamlyn Publishing Group Ltd.

Clayton, Peter. (1990). *Great Figures of Mythology.* London: Bison Books Ltd.

Cotterell, Arthur. (1986). *A Dictionary of World Mythology.* Oxford: Oxford University Press.

Coven of the Raven's Eye: Folklore. (n.d.). Raven Magick. Available from: http://home.earthlink.net/ravens.eye/id68.html .

Emperor Shibi. (n.d.). Krislon.net. Available from: http://www.krislon.net/kids/mythology/Emperor_Shibi.htm .

The Folklore of Birds. (n.d.). Available from: http://www.cottingleyglen.com/hedgewytch/bird_folklore.html .

Godwin, Malcom. (1993). *Angels: An Endangered Species.* London: Boxtree Limited.

Grimal, Pierre. (Ed.). (1965). *Larousse World Mythology.* London: Paul Hamlyn Ltd.

Ignatz Von Peczely and the Owl. (n.d.). Iridology Research. Available from: http://www.iridologyresearch.com/irihistory/page1.htm .

Jones, Alison. (1992). *Saints.* Edinburgh/New York: W & R Chambers Ltd.

Jung, Carl, et al. (1998). *Man and His Symbols.* London: Picador.

Kharitidi, Olga. (1996). *Entering the Circle.* San Francisco: HarperCollins.

Knappert, Jan. (1995). *African Mythology: An Encyclopedia of Myths and Legends.* London: Diamond Books.

Mbiti, S. John. (1975). *An Introduction to African Religion.* London: Heinemann Educational Books Ltd.

The New Encyclopaedia Britannica. (15th ed.). (1990). Chicago: Encyclopaedia Britannica Inc.

Owls in Roman Mythology. (n.d.). The Owl Pages. Available from: http://www.owlpages.com/mythology/roman.html .

Owls in English Folklore. (n.d.). The Owl Pages. Available from: http://www.owlpages.com/mythology/english.html .

Perrins, Dr. Christopher, & Harrison, Dr. C.J.O. (1979). *Birds: Their Life, Their Ways, Their World.* New York/Montreal: The Reader's Digest Association Inc.

Reed, A.W. (1965). *Myths & Legends of Australia.* Sydney: A.H. & A.W. Reed.

Simms, Eric. (1983). *A Natural History of British Birds.* London: J.M. Dent and Sons Ltd.

Spence, Lewis. (1994). *North American Indians: Myths & Legends.* London: Studio Editions Ltd.

Sykes, Egerton. (1968). *Everyman's Dictionary of Non-Classical Mythology.* London: J.M. Dent and Sons Ltd.

Tarski, Christine. (n.d.). *Fascinating Folklore of Birds: Birds Throughout the Ages.* Available from: http://www.birding.about.com/library/weekly/aa041801a.htm

Tower of London. (n.d.). Camelot Village. Available from: http://www.camelotintl.com/tower_site/ravens/legend.html .

Tucker, Suzetta. (1997-1998). *The Bestiary.* Available from: http://ww2.netnitco.net/users/legend01/dove.htm. (See also eagle, hawk, nightingale, peacock, phoenix, swan.)

Weiner, Jonathan. (1994). *The Beak of the Finch: Evolution in Real Time.* London: Random House.

The Wonder of Bird Feathers. (n.d.). Earth-Life Web Productions. Available from: http:// www.earthlife.net/birds/feathers.html .

Woodham Smith, Cecil. (1950). *Florence Nightingale.* London: Constable & Constable Ltd.

The World Book Encyclopedia. (2001). Chicago: World Book Inc.

Wright, Anne. (n.d.). *Columba: Noah's Dove.* Available from: http://www.winshop.com.au/annew/Columba.html .

Zacharias, Patricia. (n.d.). *How the Egg Came to Symbolize Easter.* Available from: http://www.detnews.com/history/easter/easter.htm .

Quotations at the beginning of chapters taken from:

Faith, Hope and Love: An Inspirational Treasury of Quotations. (1994). Philadelphia: Running Press Book Publishers.

Jeffares, Norman, A., & Gray, Martin. (Ed.). (1995). *Collins Dictionary of Quotation.* Glasgow: HarperCollins Publishers.

King James Version of the *Holy Bible.* (1977). Nashville: Thomas Nelson Publishers Inc.

Motsei, Mmatshilo. (2004). *Hearing Visions, Seeing Voices.* Bellevue: Jacana.

Shine, Betty. (1990). *Mind To Mind.* London: Corgi Books.

FINDHORN *Press*

For a complete Findhorn Press catalogue, please contact

Findhorn Press
305a The Park
Findhorn, Forres IV36 3TE
Scotland, Great Britain
tel +44 (0)1309-690582
fax + 44 (0)1309-690036
email info@findhornpress.com

or consult our website **www.findhornpress.com**